BIDDY EARLY

Biddy Early

MEDA RYAN

THE MERCIER PRESS
DUBLIN and CORK

The Mercier Press Ltd
4 Bridge Street, Cork
25 Lower Abbey Street, Dublin 1

ISBN 0 85342 551 5

FOR BOTH MY PARENTS

*There shall not be found among you. . .
an enchanter or a witch, or a charmer, or a consul-
ter with familiar spirits, or a wizard, or a necro-
mancer. For all that do these things are an abomin-
ation unto the Lord.*

Deuteronomy 18:10-12

INTRODUCTION

During my period of research for this book, I constantly came up against wide-eyed amazement: 'Do you think you should? Do you think it is alright? How well you're not afraid!' were some of the reactions. I can say now that I went through a few hair-raising moments, such as a cold wet winter's evening when I interviewed Sonny Walsh.

Up in the mountains outside Bodyke in County Clare, I had spent the evening talking to Mr Walsh about Biddy. Darkness had set in. As the night wore on he said: 'A strange thing happened. We were here one night, a few of the lads were in. We had spent the night talking about Biddy, and when they went out, the car wouldn't start. A new car, and it wouldn't start. We had to drive them home. Next day there was nothing wrong with the car. Strange!' An unusual feeling arose within me as I thought of my car outside the door. It started.

I was being reminded constantly of the many strange incidents that have occured, which people linked with Biddy; even the snags with radio and television programmes about her were set before me. Though outwardly I showed no alarm, I cannot say that I was equally calm within.

There were times when I did have a certain amount of fear (unwarranted, I know now). As I wrote this book, I sometimes had to walk away from it, but in the final analysis I was convinced that I had a task to do, and that was to write a book on Biddy Early. If only to place her in perspective, I am now glad I wrote it.

Much checking of facts has had to be done, in so far as this was possible, because of the casually kept records. The scraps of information (though sometimes quite adequate) were like pieces of a jig-saw which had to be pieced together working within the framework of the life and times of this extraordinary woman.

Meda Coughlan Ryan

CHAPTER ONE

Nestled between the Clare hills and overlooking Kilbarron Lake stands a two-room thatched cottage, once the home of a notorious woman named Biddy Early.

Arguments still persist as to whether Biddy was a witch or a person of God because she possessed powers and natural gifts beyond the comprehension of those who knew her personally. The very mention of her name in any part in Ireland, especially in County Clare, releases an astonishing flood of stories of cures, foretellings, warnings and broken spells. Her strange powers suggest to some people that she was a 'throwback' to the Firbolgs and Tuatha de Danaan, those powerful magicians who once peopled Ireland and whose last remnants took refuge in the county of Clare from the onslaught of successive invaders of Munster, according to tradition.

Biddy was born in lower Faha, a townland between Feakle and Gort, in the year 1798. This was a year in which the Irish people suffered some of the most violent and tragic events of their history, when within the space of a few weeks 30,000 people armed with pikes and pitch forks (many of them women and children) were mown down when they opposed the Crown forces in a Rebellion. Since 1169, when Ireland was first invaded by the Normans, the country had been plundered several times, and the confiscated land had been redistributed on many occasions to ordinary English soldiers and others of English birth who were given portions and estates of land taken from the native people.

Some of the best lands and houses were in the hands of landlords, often heartless and cruel, while the majority of the ordinary people of Ireland were rent-paying tenants. If rent was not forthcoming the people were evicted, their cabins burned, cattle and corn confiscated. It was into this Ireland that Biddy Early was born.

She was baptised Bridget Ellen Connors. Her mother's maiden name was Early, and for some reason this was the surname given to, or taken on by, Biddy. It is possible that 'the gift' was handed down to her from her mother which may have been the reason why she took her mother's surname. (Often the gifts of the power and knowledge to heal were handed from father to son, mother to daughter.) Her mother had a reputation, though in a limited way, as a herb-healer. When she married a local man, Tom Connors [John Thomas], people continued to call her Ellen Early, seldom using the married title of Mrs Connors.

Biddy's parents were poor, paying a weekly rent to William J. O'Brien, landlord[1] for their portion of land. She knew what it was like to go without a meal of stirabout so that they would be able to keep their mud cabin and their little holding of land on which to grow vegetables, potatoes and corn and to feed a few cows.

During these early childhood years on the farm with her parents, she went about barefooted. The clothes she wore were made by her mother from woven flax grown locally. Her greenish-blue eyes, bright red hair and fresh complexion complemented her sturdy physique.

Like other children of that time she had a good knowledge of the herbs which grew wild on the ditches, in the woods and in the fields. The curative properties of herbs were known to many during this period, and she watched her mother as she brewed and mixed herbs, which were used as cures for various pains, cuts and sores.

One of her daily tasks was to go through the fields carrying a tin gallon, which had been made by the travelling-smith, and to fill it with herbs and berries found on the ditches and to collect mosses which grew on the stones and bits of bark found loosely scattered. Her mother had shown her how to do this, explaining the value of the various herbs and plants. Following on traditional lines, many of the recipes were a family-guarded secret.

Beside a large stone in the corner of one of the fields stood another thick perpendicular stone like a block of wood jutting up to about four feet above the ground. Local tradition had it that these were put there by the fairies as they were close to a white thorn bush said to be a fairy dwelling. Biddy was regularly seen in this quiet corner where, it was said, she appeared to be talking to someone. When questioned, she would reply that she had been talking to the fairies and acquiring knowledge from them.

One day when Biddy was about ten years old her mother sent her off to a neighbour's house to collect a clocking hen, as she had some eggs to hatch. It was a mild spring day and the sun shone gently from the sky as Biddy made her way across the fields towards the neighbour's house.

About three hours later, as her mother was walking through the open half-door with a bucket of food for the hens, she saw Biddy coming empty handed towards her, and softly humming a tune.

'Where's the hen?' her mother asked.

As if in a dream Biddy looked up: 'What hen?'

'The clocking hen. Where were you?' asked her puzzled mother.

'Playing with Them,' Biddy replied.

Perhaps it was no wonder that the neighbours used to shake their head and say, 'She's a strange wan entirely!'

Indeed they sometimes asked each other the question, 'Is she one of Them?'[2]

There was a dancing master who travelled around the area, periodically visiting the townland of Faha. As was customary, he stayed the night in one of the houses in the locality and often lodged with the Connors. In company with the other boys and girls of the district Biddy learned Irish step dancing. Now a growing girl, though still barefooted, she took pleasure in mastering the intricate steps of reels and jigs, which were pounded out on the hardened-mud floor, the music being provided mainly by the on-lookers in the form of 'puss-music' or 'doodling'.

The winter evenings brought early darkness, and as a fire of turf and kindling glowed in the open hearth, neighbours gathered after the day's work. They talked of local happenings and told tales of the past and stories from other districts which they had heard in the neighbouring houses. A local poet, Brian Merriman, who cast to verse the lamentation of unmated young women and the sidhe-

court, was freely discussed when passages from
Cuirt An Mhean-Oiche were quoted at length.

Great is the boast of the Irish people
That the fairies can sit without disagreement
For two days and nights on the mountain-peak
In the mansioned palace of Lough Greany shee.[3]

The sad ending and the deeds of Crohour Higue,
another Feakle man, who was buried alive were
remembered: 'so great was his power that he was
believed to be able to charm the birds off the trees,
not only alive, but plucked and trussed ready for
the pot!'[4]

There was one story which Biddy was to recall
and retell many times during her life. One night a
few of the neighbours gathered around the hearth,
some smoking clay pipes and casting the odd spit
into the glowing fire which licked the black chimney. Only the dull light of a candle broke their
shadows as it flickered upon the wooden table
beneath the little window at the side of the cabin.

Biddy cuddled herself in a corner away from the
grown-ups as she knew from experience that she
should not pretend to understand, nor should she
ask questions of her elders. Her mother sat on the
hob, while her father sat on the wooden block at
the other side of the glowing fire.

'Jack, the cobler' pushed back his cap over his
greying hair, and began to tell his tale:

Not long ago there was a woman by name Moll
Anthony, living near the Red Hills in County
Kildare. It was said she was in league with the
fairies, and they charmed her with cures. This is
the truth I'm telling ye, for she has a son abroad
there today, by name Jack. He's a class of a cow-

11

doctor. Anyway in her time crowds came to her cabin looking for help and advice for any sickness or misfortune of one kind or another. 'Pon my soul, that's the kind of thing she did. Fairy-doctor were the words they called her. She was in the habit of putting some secret stuff in a bottle and told the person who was sick or came to her, 'Don't fall asleep on the way home.'

Begor anyway there was one young woman who had travelled from a neighbouring county to consult this Moll Anthony woman. A relative of hers was very ill. Moll gave her the magic drop in the bottle and said, 'Keep your eyes open on the way home.'

Anam 'on diabhal, after she had walked a good part of the journey, didn't she get woeful tired. Down she sat by the side of a ditch to take her ease a bit, but 'twasn't long until the sleep overcame her. Then she had this almighty dream. A wrinkled old hag, her teeth gone, with a beak nose and a fierce scowl came towards her as if to clutch her in her long skinny arms. The young woman gave an almighty roar of terror, jumped on her feet and as she did so, the magic bottle fell to the ground, and was broken in little pieces on the stones.

'Tis said that the hideous hag of her dream was a spirit from the other world with whom Moll Anthony was said to be in league. Anyway to finish the story, when the young woman got home, she found her sick relative dead in the bed.[5]

CHAPTER TWO

Biddy was the only girl in the Connors family. There is mention of a brother Paddy whom it was said had been taken away, meaning that either he died or the fairies took him, it being believed that the fairies had this great power. If the 'good people' wanted a child for one of their own women who had suffered a mishap, they took a human child. A mother who was taken at child-birth, it was understood, was wanted to nurse one of the 'earth children'.

As was the case with most of the neighbouring children, Biddy got little formal schooling. Her daily language was Irish but she spoke what was to most people the foreign language of English. Many of the people of Ireland knew that in order to get a good position (though most were not open to them because of their religion) one had to be freely acquainted with the language of their landlords and/or oppressors. These rulers had begun to insist that English was to be the spoken tongue.

Biddy's parents could neither read nor write; but they believed in the power of the Almighty. Kneeling on the cold floor at nightfall with their daughter, after a simple meal of potatoes with salt and milk, they thanked Him through the Rosary for getting them through another day.

The young girl had heard stories of injustices towards many who openly defended their religion, because there was no freedom for Irish Catholics. Many bishops and regular clergy had left the country after the 1697 Banishment Act, and had been forbidden to return under the penalty of death for high treason. Some diocesan priests remained but they dared not speak out against injustices by the ruling class. By the time Biddy was a girl of thirteen, the clergy had regained their status amongst the peasants and had acquired a place as figures of power.

A young woman came to the Connors' house one evening as darkness was beginning to set in. Homeless, she wandered through the county seeking a bite to eat and a place to rest her head for the night. Biddy's mother who had a warm heart invited her in. 'You're welcome to share what we've got for the night,' she said.

As the night wore on, the meal had been eaten, the prayers over, some neighbours began to come on *cuaird* and storytelling commenced. They learned from the woman that she was from outside Nenagh in County Tipperary. Naturally they all wondered why she walked the roads.

'I am without a cabin,' she told them, and almost broke into tears as she told them that she was unable to pay the rent.

'They came one night and burned us out. The scuffle was terrible. My Paddy was killed. Wicked they were, that crowbar gang.'

She explained that she had two children to take with her that night after the eviction. With only the sky as a roof she watched her three week's old son die in her arms, and she later buried him on the roadside, digging the clay with her bare hands.

'Then there was only me and Johnny. The poor

garsoon, we used to be travelling. But he got the fever. . . I do be thinking about it all, as I walk the roads.'[6]

Young Biddy never forgot this. She had heard first hand the hardship of an eviction, and she was to remember this incident in later years when she came face to face with a landlord.

The young woman also told about a man who had nine children. When one got sick he went to the priest and begged him for a cure.

'You must leave him to the mercy of the Almighty God,' the priest had said. The woman continued, 'Wasn't that a hard thing to say, and him having a house full of children. He could cure him if he wanted to. He had the power.'

Pishogues went hand in hand with the daily life of the people of rural Ireland during the eighteenth and nineteenth centuries. Many parents considered it a curse rather than a blessing when a girl was born with red hair which was thought to be unlucky as Judas was said to have had red hair. It made little difference that this colouring was rampant along the western seaboard, mainly due to the earlier inter-marrying with settlers from Scandinvavian countries. It was said, 'If you meet a woman with red hair first thing in the morning, take three steps backwards, otherwise you will have bad luck for the rest of the day.' They told each other to 'beware of the red haired woman who enters your house while you churn the butter, if she does not put her hand on the churn after entering, she will take the butter from you.'

Biddy rather enjoyed the fact that her red hair, which she sometimes put in a single thick tress down the centre of her back, was a cause for alarm by some people.

She knew from an early age that she was somebody to be reckoned with; and people wondered about her fondness for wandering off to her fairy place. She had heard them talk about her, and this gave her a certain sense of pride. Though Biddy's parents were concerned about her actions, still they didn't worry unduly, as she was always pleasant, good humoured and hummed quite a lot. She also noticed that she was aware of things which were about to occur. One evening Biddy asked her mother if she was not feeling well, and that night her mother got very ill.

By now Biddy was able to do most of the work, feeding hens, milking cows, washing and beating clothes by the stream, just as her mother had been doing for years.

As the days went by she found she had to take her mother's place more often, because her strength appeared to be failing. Each week, this undernourished woman was spending more time in bed. The herb mixtures which she forced herself to take were apparently not doing her any good.

Then one cold winter's evening as the wind howled around the cabin, her mother died.

Biddy was just sixteen years of age.

CHAPTER THREE

During the spring of 1814, Biddy worked hard, bringing in creels of turf and doing all the household chores, always trying to stretch the food as far as possible, while her father toiled in the fields in an effort to continue to pay the rent. Though he was a strong man her father was afraid that they might be unable to hold on to the place because the rent had been raised once again and the landlord showed little mercy to those whose payments were not forthcoming. When her mother was alive she had received little gifts of food in return for her herb mixtures, but Biddy was not so successful. Because of her strange behaviour, the neighbours did not trust her 'concoctions' and were not willing to accept the brews which she made up for curative purposes. She, knowing that the time had not come, accepted their reactions without a murmur.

During this period after her mother's death, she found consolation once more in her fairy corner. There she was alone with her thoughts, or indeed alone with her friends, as she said herself. It has been reported that one evening her mother appeared to her and told her not to be afraid.

She was out near the ditch behind the house. Biddy believed that the dead could come back to you if you wished it. Anyway when she appeared to her, she told her daughter about a bottle which would help her throughout her life,

17

she said: 'When you will be twenty-one, you will be able to use the bottle to do good for people. Don't tell this secret to anyone until you have become of age.'[7]

She did indeed later acquire her bottle although its origin is uncertain.

Biddy would sit on a stump of wood outside the open doorway in summertime and brush her long bright red hair while she hummed gently to herself. Neighbours frowned on the idea that a young girl should be heard humming or singing during the first year after her mother's death. 'Gone in the head,' they would remark. Being thoroughly aware of what people were saying, she had by this time given up telling about her conversations with 'the good people' and was beginning to turn her thoughts inwards. Her strange beauty also lent itself to local gossip, especially the red glow which filled her eyes when caught in the glimmer of a candle light.

One evening when her father returned from the field, he said that he was not feeling too well. Perspiration covered his body as he lay on his homemade bed. This frightened Biddy, as she knew that he had not long to live. He had 'the fever'. Within a few days he was dead. And as he was laid to rest six months after his wife and the clay was shovelled over his coffin, the young girl was aware that she was without a real human companion.

It was not possible for her to remain on in the cabin as she was unable to pay the rent. She had no alternative but to go to relatives who lived further north in Slieveanore, a childless couple who had no time for the folly of a young girl who talked to the fairies. Though it was common belief in the neighbourhood that many people had seen spirits or fairies—this was the subject of many a fireside conversation—they were heard to say that Biddy's actions were *gan braon ciall*.[8] They also could not understand how she could know of things before they happened and began to suspect that she was in league with some evil being.

Constant battles arose between them, and blame was cast on her dead mother, as well as on her red hair which the woman of the house threatened to cut. One day after Biddy took a trip back to her fairy place, the woman gave her so much abuse that she left early one morning while the couple were still sleeping.

She then travelled the roads. Little is known of her adventures at this point, though it is written, 'that she wandered around for some months working here and there for her keep'.[9] Eventually she found what appeared to be secure domestic employment on a Clare estate owned by a Limerick landlord named Sheehy. On this estate, in the townland of Carheen,[10] Biddy lived in one of the cottages, paying a high rent like the other tenants. Though her dwelling was called a cottage, it was in fact a hovel, just a one-room, low-thatched cabin, sparsely furnished with a 'make-shift' bed, a little table and chair and a few pieces of crockery.

As a domestic servant in the Sheehy mansion, she had to work hard for little pay. She was given all the lower jobs: washing floors, scrubbing the tables until the clear grain of the timber was visible, and doing the same to the solid wooden chairs in the kitchen quarters. In the part of the house where her unmarried master lived, she had to polish and dust the contents of 'the big rooms'. Often he would abuse her, treating her like one of his animals (in fact less well because he was rather kind to his horses and dogs) if something was not to his satisfaction.

Though she was an intelligent girl and quick with her tongue, she had not yet learned to read or write. One of the male workers, a labourer on the estate and the son of a travelling-schoolmaster, agreed to teach her. During the weeks which followed Tom, who had some books, came to her cabin at night time. He had worked in the fields all day while she worked hard in 'the big house'. Painstakingly, he explained to her how a language could be read. She was a bright pupil, eager to learn.

'You can do it,' he used to say, *'Níl sé ró dheacair.'*

Eventually she was able to read, although it is not known if she ever learned to write; it is commonly believed that she did not.

It was about this time that she began to acquire a reputation as a herbalist. She had a natural cure for almost every common ailment, gathering the local herbs, flowers, barks and mosses from which she brewed her potions. Such a work was an art requiring great skill and knowledge, as herbs had to be picked and stewed at different stages of growth, and at certain times of the year, if they were to be effective. Following on tradition she did not betray her mother's confidence but kept well-guarded the secret recipes which had been passed down through many generations.

She kept these mixtures in various bottles, and gave potions to people who called for a cure for a friend or relative who lay sick. Invariably she warned her customer against any potential attack on the way home: 'As you near the Black Wood, your horse will take fright. Take care not to be thrown.

And be extra careful that this bottle is not broken.'[11]

By the winter of 1816 Biddy had been almost eighteen months in Carheen, and during this time her landlord had repeatedly raised the rent. Like the other tenants living in the hovels on the estate, she found it difficult to keep up the payments, so they banded together to petition the landlord for a just rent. This did not find favour with her master. For conspiring with the other tenants in this effort to attain fair rents, she was evicted. At the outset she opposed the eviction but when a court order followed, she knew it was futile to resist any further.

It was a cold winter's morning when Sheehy arrived with his henchmen to evict her. Biddy stood in the doorway, her long red hair piled high on her head, looked towards the well-dressed master on horseback and said, 'You Sheehy, your bones shall not be found to receive a Christian burial, but even I shall be laid to rest on hallowed ground.'[12]

That night three other tenants who had been evicted in the morning, aided by a local small holder named Touhy, made their way with lighted coals towards the master's large house. On their way they met one of the maids, Nell Canny, and feared she would betray them, despite the fact that Biddy had previously told them this would happen. 'Don't harm her. Leave her alone, she could be useful,' Biddy had said.

The men murdered Sheehy that night, and burned his house around his dead body. No trace of his remains were ever found.[13]

Subsequently one of the men, Touhy, was arrested on the evidence of a burned patch of grass outside his hall door. When he was being tried in

Limerick Court, Nell Canny, who was present, asked for permission to say a few words.

'Twas I dropped that coal,' she said. 'I was bringing it from Mr Touhy's house to light my master's fire.'

When the case concluded, there was not sufficient evidence to convict Touhy, so he was released.[14]

CHAPTER FOUR

The year was 1817. Biddy was travelling the roads yet again in search of a bit to eat and a bed to lie on, not something which found favour with her. It was a harsh reminder of the evicted woman who visited her home when she was a child.

The rough stone roads and pathways and the cold harsh weather of January and February made hard walking. There was poverty everywhere, so getting a steady job was difficult. She carried many a stone water-jar on her head, she handled and carted turf for the big houses and scrubbed floors to get a morsel of food and perhaps a bed of hay in the stable at night. Peasant women were beasts of burden, too poor to grumble.

There were some simple folk on whom she called and they, as her own family had been, were willing to share what they had. Biddy was a sensitive person, however, and knew the people had little, so she did not like to call on them except when caught by nightfall without shelter.

After wandering for quite some time, Biddy eventually reached Ennis. Weary of the road, carrying only the clothes on her back, weak and tired of the struggle, she made her way to a workhouse known as the House of Industry.[15] This large stone building was built by private subscription in 1776 for the 'helpless poor, and for keeping in restraint sturdy beggars and vagabonds. . . Power was given to the corporations to grant badges to such of the helpless poor as had resided one year in their respective counties, cities or towns, with a licence to beg within such limits and for such time as might be thought fit. . . '[16]

Although she was glad to have a roof over her head each night and some portion of food to quell the rattles in her stomach, Biddy found life within its walls depressing.

Soup was boiled in big pots and dished out roughly. The inmates were often herded along like cattle and for Biddy, who was intelligent and individualistic, life was difficult to bear. Like all the others, she had to work for her daily keep, scrubbing floors, washing clothes, drawing water and washing and peeling potatoes—difficult tasks for the undernourished, and made all the more unpleasant since the bosses and overseers were, for the most part, cruel and demanding.

One day Biddy had just scrubbed the rough stone hall floor, got up off her knees and was about to take the bucket of dirty water when one of the head-warders came along. He purposely knocked over the bucket, scattering the filthy water in many directions. 'Why don't you get the fairies to wipe it up for you?' he hissed.[17]

She was extremely upset. Obviously stories about her had been circulating. Cold and wet she knew there was no alternative but to mop it up silently.

There was one incident which saddened her very much. Among the inmates, there was a girl, barely sixteen, whose parents had died and who was alone like herself. One day the girl got into trouble when she was unable to carry some heavy load. The warder was harshly abusing her when Biddy intervened and as a result Biddy's pride and glory, her beautiful red hair, was cut. 'This will teach you to remember where you are,' she was told.[18]

In order to get away from the filth, poverty and abuse of this institution, she started to make trips, whenever possible, to the fairs and the *fleadhanna* in the surrounding towns and villages.

The fair was a gathering place where there was singing and storytelling; clothes and food were sold; musicians and poets gathered; clowns, tricksters, and jugglers entertained; and cattle and horses were sold and the deal finally clinched with a spit on the palm. These places of assembly were frequented by both males and females. Drinking was part of the entertainment, and many a man returned home to his wife, drunk from whiskey or the illicit spirits, which was distilled locally, and called poteen.[19]

Biddy liked the variety in spite of the fact that she had no money to spend; and as time went by, she made a point of getting out of the House of Industry, which smelt of poverty, in the hope that she would find employment.

On one such occasion while visiting a fair in Tulla, Biddy saw a local faction fight. Certain families would fight other families, or a faction from a district faced its rival from another area in a battle of stick fighting (Irish fencing). The ash plant or blackthorn stick used for this purpose was chosen and prepared with care. The knocking of a stick from the grasp of his opponent was a skill acquired by the expert fighter, and 'the getting' of his man was all part of faction fighting. There were times when men were badly injured and sometimes a death occurred at this type of game.

Biddy watched a woman trail her coat in front

of an opposing group; a tall young boy stood on it and the challenge was taken up. It was considered a disgrace if the day passed without a blow being struck. Biddy did not like violence, and cringed at such a sport. However as she watched the fate of the young man who was now joined by others, she saw an eager, older man beside her. After a time she spoke to him, and discovered that it was his son who had led the fight. The father anxious that his faction would win, urged on the son with shouts of encouragement. Unintentionally, she found herself taking sides.

As time wore on, the young man's faction eventually drove their opponents back, and many had to run.

Biddy learned that the man beside her was Pat Malley from Gurteenreagh,[20] Feakle, a widower with a comfortable size holding. The pair chatted, and afterwards they walked around to see the 'Chaney Sellers' with their stock of jugs, bowls and vessels.

Pat Malley, being a local was well known, paused from time to time for a chat with neighbours, and was proud to have such a good looking girl by his side. She met his only son, John, who had earlier been involved in the faction fight, and a few days later when she again met Pat Malley at Tulla fair, he offered her employment. She willing accepted as she was glad to leave the degrading 'Poor House'.

Now in her early twenties, she proved a good companion and housekeeper for Pat. At night when the neighbours came visiting and the story-telling around the fireside began, this good looking girl was the centre of attraction among the men folk; they treated her as an equal, which was something she had not so far experienced in adult life. As the weeks and months went by, she had adjusted to life at Gureenreagh and fitted well into the homestead. Pat had grown to like Biddy, and after six months he asked her to marry him.

Most marriages were the product of match-making, where often the father made a match for his daughter without her consent, age making no difference. There was always a dowry given in the form of cattle, horses, or other farm property. Biddy was being taken without any dowry, so she was glad to say 'yes' to the proposal of marriage, even though Pat, a widower, was more than twice her age.

Biddy married Pat Malley, a tall, good looking man with dark receding hair, generally wearing a cap, and homespun trousers and jacket, in Feakle Parish Church. Nothing is known of the celebration which followed, though it is likely that this was held in Pat's house. It would be a big day for the neighbours who would all gather, bringing with them food and drink to have full and plenty on a wedding day. It was customary not to let the bride feel she would have to live in a house which had not sufficient. It was a day for celebration, singing, dancing, storytelling and drinking, until the couple had retired for their first night together.

The new bride at Gurteenreagh had at last obtained security and happiness, if only for a few short years, before she became a controversial figure.

CHAPTER FIVE

Pat Malley's wife continued to be known as Biddy Early. Having spent many difficult years, she was now a farmer's wife and mistress of her own simple home — a three-room thatched cabin. The stones and clay used in its building and the rushes for the thatch had all come from the neighbouring hills and valleys. The turf was cut in the local bogs and its smoke wound its way up the chimney or filled the cabin with fumes.

At Gurteenreagh, like most farmers' wives in the district, Biddy kept hens, and reared chickens. It was a rare treat to have meat for a meal, but when the hens grew old and were no longer capable of producing eggs, they were killed and boiled in a pot — which the local blacksmith had made — and it hung on a crane over the fire of turf and 'kippens'. For the most part the meals were simple, as the farm produce had to be sold to pay the rent and to buy the necessities of life. If any improvement was done on the holding, the landlord was likely to increase his rent demand, so no farmer was inclined to better his methods. Indeed Biddy had been well aware of this insecurity from early childhood.

Periodically she took a trip to the fair in Tulla, but generally she travelled to the local market of Feakle with her eggs and butter.

Preparing the butter for market and taking care of the hens was 'woman's territory' and these tasks were surrounded by many pishogues. For example, if a woman took an egg from her neighbour's basket, she would be taking the luck of the laying hens for the coming year. It was considered wise to leave one egg from the hatch for the fairies. But if anyone found bad eggs in her garden, they were considered to have been put there by a neighbour who wanted to transfer her family's ill-luck.

When Biddy visited town or market, she was always neatly dressed, wearing a gently flaired grey homespun skirt falling to ankle length from a gathered waist band, and topped by a homespun, long sleeve blouse. The shawl which she wore over her shoulders was caught by a broach or pin over her bosom. Though small in stature, she carried herself well.[21]

Biddy was well able to make stirabout or hasty pudding which was a mixture of maize and milk boiled to a thick consistency; she could make a cake with the 'yella meal' and she sometimes boiled cabbage or nettle leaves to accompany the potatoes.

As well as cooking meals, she continued brewing herbs which she used for cures for animals, friends and relatives.

She chopped finely leaves from cabbage, stinging nettle, and some watercress; these she bound together with a stiffly beaten egg white, sprinkled other addatives, exactly as her mother had, and used it as a poultice for many a swollen leg, arm or shoulder. She used mixtures that nobody knew, instinctively aware of the correct amount of herb or plant needed for a particular ailment. She knew every plant and its properties and, as time passed, became more aware, through experimentation, of how they should be mixed and blended.[22]

Gradually people began to tell each other how helpful she had been in curing a member of the family. 'When I went to Biddy Early's one day, she told me that my son was worse than what I was,' said Mrs Clancy. 'She told me to take what I had been taking before — the dandelions. I did, and here I am. As to my son, she gave me a bottle of some mixture, and now he's better.'[23]

Word went round that she could prevent further misfortunes.

A man named John Mac Donnagh had some cattle and young calves. Three of his calves died after each other, and so he buried them in his field. Then another got sick; he decided to go to Biddy Early. He had no good shirt, so he borrowed one from a neighbour. But when Biddy saw him coming, she said, 'Here you are coming with your borrowed shirt on you, and you are after burying three calves, and you left another sick at home, and he is dead now.' Then she said, 'Let him die.' And when he got home, right enough, the calf was dead, but none of his cattle died after that.[24]

Biddy was now quite happy and accepted her lot with this older man, Pat Malley; she soon bore him a son. (Some writings say that there were two more children born to her from this marriage but the facts are not quite clear as there doesn't appear to be any further mention of these children. There was definitely the one son.)

She had found security, happiness and a real home for the first time since early childhood. Having had to fend for herself from an early age made her appreciate all the more the value of human contact and love. Certainly Pat appreciated her value as a wife and was proud of the fame which she was gaining. Unfortunately he drank more than was good for him, because the house was never without bottles of poteen which people brought as gifts in return for cures.

After five years her husband got sick, an illness which proved fatal and within a week he was dead. At twenty-five years of age, Biddy was a widow.

Biddy was not the type of person to remain in mourning for long. She was a good looking woman, living in a house with her stepson John, and it was no secret that the two got on well together. He was near her own age and had tended to confide in her, looking on her as a good friend rather than a step-mother, so it was only natural that she married him a short time after the death of his father, her first husband. In this way, her own future and that of her son was guaranteed, as she continued to be mistress of the house at Gurteenreagh.

CHAPTER SIX

It was during the year 1822 that the incident known as 'the Royal Visit' occurred.[25] One day a gypsy 'queen' seeking help visited Biddy. This was, of course, considered a great honour and she was very elevated to be placed in such high esteem.

This 'queen' came from County Kerry, and not wishing her family or tribe to know of the visit, travelled *incognito*. She was extremely pleased with Biddy who was able to converse in Shelta, a secret jargon used for many generations by Irish tinkers, gypsies, beggars and pipers.

Hall dschal coa? ('How are you?')
Latscho coa scha mange. ('I am well.')
Ho hie tu? ('What is the matter?')

It is reported that Biddy helped her successfully and that the 'queen', being highly pleased, rewarded Biddy by giving her a secret herbal recipe to be used as a pain killer. This she accepted with gratitude, used and valued it as a prized possession. Knowing what would happen in the future was common to both, and much of their conversation centered around this. She never forgot the visit and often spoke of it as the years went on. She never betrayed the 'queen's' confidence and nobody was ever told the contents of her problem or request.

The fame of Biddy Early as a healer had spread throughout the country. Many notable people were already calling on her. Daniel O'Connell, who was about to seek election as a candidate for Clare in 1828, went to her for advice. Naturally she felt it a great honour to be so highly regarded. As always she respected the confidence placed on her and never revealed to anybody the contents of the meeting.

Public voting took place in Ennis Courthouse and lasted a week. Parishioners from each district were led by their priests. Fr McInerney of Feakle led a group of freeholders to the voting venue, 'carrying green boughs, and music before them.' Even though at this time, priests were beginning to look askance at Biddy's activities, still, it is said, she encouraged the people to follow their priest. And in doing so they brought not only success to their own county Clare, but also to the Irish people, because O'Connell defeated his opponent Vesey Fitzgerald by a majority of 982 votes.

Moss had many curative properties and Biddy was openly seen picking bits of this tufty growth from around the wheel of the mill-stream of Bally-lee, beside the Tower where W. B. Yeats came to live later.

According to Dolly Steward:

For the common ailments such as a bad cold or falling hair, Biddy would brew some tea from cat mint, that little plant which grows wild almost everywhere, and in every marshy spot by lake or river. A cure for sore throats or tightness of the chest, would be made with little or no trouble from the common turnip; and whooping cough she could cure with thyme tea. The plaintain, growing in every ditch, is one of the most healing of all herbs, and in the Highlands of Scotland it is called 'Slanlus' which means, the healing plant. Nettles, potatoes, apples, honey, all these things were plentiful and could be used as cures for all kinds of ailments.[26]

It is reported that Biddy seldom took money (some say she never took it) in return for any favours which she granted, but was always willing to accept gifts in kind — the decision of giving rested entirely with the receiver.

The acceptance, however, rested with Biddy:

People going to Biddy Early for a favour would sometimes take a hen. A woman who was going to her went out to get a hen. The first hen she caught was a fine fat one, and she said: 'the devil a one of her will get you'. And she got another hen. The hen she got this time was one whose bones were out through her. Then she put on her fine plaid shawl, and gave the road a welt. When she came to Biddy's house, Biddy said, 'Why didn't you bring the first hen your caught? I know well why you didn't bring her, you thought she was too fat. Well you can go about your business now, and leg it home as quick as you came. As long as you begrudged to give me the fat hen, I'll begrudge to give you a cure.'[27]

Not alone was Biddy noted for her power of healing, but she was also fast becoming recognised as a woman with some special gift, that of knowing in advance the course of certain events. And because of this, people began to speak of her as 'The Wise Woman'. They sought her advice as well as her help on occasions, and did exactly as she commanded.

A sister of my mother lived in Moher and she was very sick. My mother was coming from Ennis and she went to see her.

'Well,' says my mother, 'why don't you send for Biddy Early?'

'We don't know her, maybe you'd go.'

My mother went and I went with her. She knew what brought us as soon as we arrived.

'You're welcome,' says she to my mother, 'but I'm afraid you're late in the business you're coming about. Why didn't you come sooner?' says she. 'And by-the-way, why isn't it one o' themselves that came to me? 'Twas one o' themselves had a right to come and not you.'

'Well,' she said, 'that sick woman will be buried on such a day,' naming the day, 'and let you not go to the funeral.'

'Twas true for her, the woman, my aunt, was buried on the day she said, and my mother did not go to the funeral. She kept Biddy's advice.[28]

Biddy had a rare gift of sensing trouble. If somebody had a problem and approached her, she discovered that she was receptive to the situation, even before the person spoke. She worked on this, and the more people who came to her, the more experience she was gaining.

A man from Ballykenny had sheep stolen from him, so he decided to go to Biddy Early. When he went to her she knew what he wanted before he asked her, and she told him they were stolen by a man who lived at the side of the river; that he wore a white corduroy trousers, and that he sold the sheep at the fair of Charleville yesterday morning, and took sail for America. She told the man that he had a wound there in his shin, and that there was a little trouble in store for him, and he would have letters. Soon after that his brother died.[29]

Michael O'Brien wanted to see what she was like; he went to her, and she said, 'How are you, Michael O'Brien, and how are you all in Coolcappa?' She seemed to know so much about him that he left and did not ask her any questions which he had intended about his future business, and he never went back to her.[30]

CHAPTER SEVEN

Life at the Gurteenreagh homestead was changing; people with problems from far and near were calling at various times of the day and night. Family life was disrupted for Biddy and her husband. Though she was enjoying the increasing fame, her husband was over-indulging in the extra drink which continued to be brought by well-wishers to the house.

Some years after her second marriage, her son Paddy left home and did not return for a period of seven years. It was rumoured locally that he was a changeling, one of the fairy folk, and was called to return.

In the cabin at night, when the day's work was over, the young men in the neighbourhood came to play cards, to talk and also to drink. John helped himself to the spirits, not alone during these hours of relaxation but also during his erratic working day, erratic because he was no longer capable of putting in a full working day.

The constant drinking of alcohol, especially the low grade whiskey and illegally distilled poteen, was gradually injuring her husband's health. In spite of her warning he continued to drink. He was seldom boisterous due to over-indulging; rather, it tended to make him quiet and sombre. Gradually he developed a liver ailment, from which he died in 1840.

Biddy was a widow for a second time and she was lonely.

Then one day her son came back to her, but he was completely changed. He was not inclined to work or help her in any way. He spent much time in bed, smoked a strong clay pipe behind her back, and when she was away from home, travelled into the village to meet the local lads. Although he tried to fool her by stealing back to bed before she returned, she always knew, but cast a mother's blind eye towards all his misdeeds. She overlooked many of his shortcomings because of his skill at hurling and the stories of his successes which delighted her.

She was often alone with her own thoughts and enjoyed developing the power of her mind, but she continually craved for human contact and often she would leave her home, with her son in charge, and journey through the surrounding countryside.

On one such ocasion she was in the Enistymon area, near nightfall, and as she was not far from the home of a friend, she decided to call on him and ask if she might stay the night. He had recently married, and when Biddy knocked at the door, it was his wife who answered it. Biddy introduced herself, told her what she wanted, and asked if she might come in. The young woman, knowing Biddy's reputation, was reluctant to allow such a notorious character into her home, so she refused saying she had no spare room and could not possibly put her up for the night.

Biddy then described to the young woman a room which was at the back of the house, containing a stretcher bed.

'That room will suit me fine,' she said, 'though

there are some panes missing from the window, and broken widow panes let in strange things that we would be better without.'

Thoroughly scared, the young woman, seeing no option, invited her in because she had a room exactly as Biddy had described it, stretcher bed, broken panes and all. So Biddy was successful in getting her night's lodgings.[31]

Soon she met a man named Tom Flannery to whom, though considerably younger than herself, she took an immediate liking. A labourer and a native of Finley, Quinn, Co. Clare, Tom was a fine, tall, good-looking, dark-haired boy. Not being the type of woman who would waste much time in a long courtship, the pair were married after only a short acquaintance. As with her previous husbands, marriage did not alter her name; Biddy Early was the woman people knew.

She left the farm at Gurteenreagh to her son (though basically it all depended on whether he could pay the rent) and moved with her husband to a little two-room cottage on Dromore Hill, over-looking a lake which later became known as Biddy Early's lake.[32] And just below on the roadside, a spring well with a never ending supply provided water for the house.[33]

Her new home was reached by a path which rose slantwise from the road, turned sharply at the top, and ran straight to the door of the thatched mud-walled cabin. The living quarters contained a dresser, a few *súgán* chairs, a wooden table, a settle and, the focal point, an open fireplace which was instantly visible over the half-door. The little bedroom was sparsely furnished; it contained only a bed, a chair and some open shelving.

It is this home at Kilbarron[34] which is identified with the name of Biddy Early 'The Healer', 'The Wise Woman', 'The Witch'. Here she found love, comfort and success, as well as controversy, hostility and abuse. It was after her settling at Kilbarron that it became commonly known that she had a 'magic' bottle.

The truth as to how Biddy obtained the bottle has not been ascertained, and many are the stories which are told about it. One account goes that, around 1817, she worked for a short period for John Browne of Bruff where the Catholic section of a mixed Protestant and Catholic graveyard was being lowered. Earth was being drawn by Brown's horse and butt to one of his fields. None of his labourers would shovel the earth, believing that trouble would follow, so Biddy agreed to give a hand. It was while doing so, local tradition holds, that she found her bottle.[35]

According to a ballad, composed during her lifetime:

In '41 when her first born son
   Played a fairy game of hurley
I tell you true that the Bottle o' Blue
   Was given to Biddy Early.

The most popular account relates that the bottle was given to her by her son Paddy.

Paddy was a noted hurler in the locality, and one evening when returning home from a game near Scariff, and nearing Feakle, he was surprised to see a group of men preparing for a hurling match. Surprised, because he did not recognise any of the players since he knew all the young men in the district, especially the hurlers, for

40

miles around.

One of the players approached him and asked him to make up their number as they were one man short. Although feeling tired, obligingly Paddy jumped down into the field and played a strong game, his side winning the contest.

Nobody spoke until he had climbed on to the road again. Then one of the strangers whom Paddy now strongly believed to be earth folk or fairy men, called him back and handed him a dark glass bottle, and said, 'We thank you, take this and give it to your mother, she will know what to do with it.'

The young lad turned away and gingerly holding the bottle started on his journey to his mother's home. As an afterthought he turned to ask the donor whom he should say had given it to him, but to his astonishment the field was empty. He was shaken and rather frightened, but clutching the bottle he quickened his pace, and arrived safely at Kilbarron, giving it to his mother, he told her what had occurred on the Scariff road. She was delighted to receive this endowment from Mother Nature, and gazed fixedly into it, seeing certain omens and portents which were of meaning to her.[36]

Disagreements often arise as to whether the bottle was blue or black; the exact colour is disputed but, apparently, it was dark. It became the subject of intense interest, curiosity, superstition and conjecture. The bottle, which stood about nine inches in height with a six-inch stem which tapered into a bulbous shape in the lower part, was carefully guarded by Biddy, who always wrapped it in a red cloth.

Yet another account of how Biddy acquired her dark bottle tells that one day she was left minding a delicate child by his parents. The child was not young but had never left the cradle, and the local people believed he was a changeling. During the afternoon, the child asked Biddy to take down the fiddle which hung on the wall hook. She did as requested, whereupon the child began to play strange sweet music.

Biddy listened. After some time playing the child handed back the fiddle to her.

'Hang up the fiddle again,' he said. When she had this done, he spoke softly to her, 'I won't live long. Take that bottle from the cleby [shelf over the fireplace]. It will give you power. Be sure to do good with it.'[37]

Perhaps one of the best known stories of the bottle concerns a relative of Biddy's who had an inordinate love of dancing. When he was stopped at the cross-roads one night by some strangers and asked if he would accompany them to a dance, he did so without hesitation, wondering to himself how a dance could have been organised so near home without his having been aware of it.

To his astonishment, his new found friends brought him across fields to a disused house where there were a number of people standing in a circle mocking a pale beautiful girl, and after watching for some time, to his horror he saw she was deaf, blind and dumb. He was filled with pity for her and wondered how he could rescue her from her tormentors.

Suddenly a cock crowed and the fairy host, for such it was, vanished, leaving the girl standing

42

in the middle of the floor. The young man guided her home and the following night he again went to the empty house hoping that he might by some good fortune learn of some way of breaking the spell which he was convinced had been placed on the girl. His vigil had its reward. The fairies returned at nightfall and fell to lamenting the loss of the butt of their fun whom they had hoped to find still there, as they knew she could never get away by herself. One fairy woman, more kind-hearted than the rest said, that she had brought along a bottle, three drops of which would have cured her.

Eventually he succeeded in getting the bottle and hurried home with it. He touched the girls eyes, ears and tongue with a drop of the liquid, and to his great delight the girl stood cured before him. Next day he brought her home to her father, who was a rich Limerick merchant. He was overjoyed to have his daughter restored to him.

Soon the gallant rescuer married the lovely girl and lived happily. Having no further need of the bottle, he took it to his cousin Biddy whom he knew would be able to use it to do good.[38]

Though different stories were related as to how she got the bottle, Biddy herself never told anybody how she acquired it, but she never put it too far out of reach. When she travelled anywhere away from home, she held it firmly, close to her body, out of public view beneath her shawl.

At home in Kilbarron, she kept the wrapped bottle in the middle drawer of the dresser, which stood just inside the window of her little kitchen.

CHAPTER EIGHT

People believe that Biddy could reveal what was hidden beneath the shadows of the past; that she could see down the vistas of the future; that she could tell the whereabouts of things lost or hidden; and that she could effect cures. In all cases she referred to a magic bottle, and read from it the required information. She frequently mystified her visitors by addressing them familiarly by their names, though she might never have seen them before, and by referring to matters which they had always considered close family secrets. She succeeded in playing upon the credulity and superstition of the peasantry to an enormous extent, hundreds of people from all parts of the country visiting her each year.[39]

Biddy used the bottle as her talisman, generally though not always referring to it when she wished to know about her subject in more depth.

The district around Feakle was a well known flax growing area so Biddy used the mucilanginous seeds of the plant to advantage in the making of poultices useful for festering fingers, or other minor cuts.[40]

As had been her practice since her early days on the Sheely estate, Biddy nearly always gave her caller 'a potion' of some substance in a little bottle to take home to the sick person, that is if the patient was unable to come to her. When handing over the little bottle, she invariably warned not to let it fall. 'Be careful don't break it,' she would say. 'Look out when crossing the humpy bridge, the horse may stumble.' She would sometimes state, 'You'll never bring that bottle home,' and he wouldn't. When this happened the sick person got worse and generally died or in some cases, was dead when the traveller arrived home.

I remember when I was a young girl, a man called Tommy Leamy came to our house, and I heard him telling my mother this story: I will tell it as he told it.

I had a son. One day I had a tub of boiling water in the middle of the floor, the lad was young and he backed into it and got scalded. I was advised to go to Biddy Early as quick as I could, but I had no money only half-a-crown, and so I went to a neighbour, and got five shillings from them, then I had seven and six in all. Off I went to Feakle 'cross the mountains, and as soon as I landed in Kilbarron I went to Biddy, and of course she knew all, before ever I opened my mouth. She went into the room then and looked through a big bottle she had. Then she went and made up a bottle for me, and when she was handing me the bottle I went to give her the seven and six.

'Keep the five shillings,' she said, 'that you got from your neighbour, and when you go home give them back their money.'

So off I went with the bottle in my pocket, and the very minute I left her door, nothing began to bother me except the son at home, and I was half running to get home on time. But

45

with the dint of worry that was on me, didn't I forget all about the advice I got, and as soon as I reached the style, in with me across it, I hadn't gone ten yards when I fell and broke the bottle. 'Twas then I thought of myself, but I was too late. The harm was done. When I reached home he was very bad, and the poor child got a bad turn that night, and he was dead before morning.

I suppose that it was allotted for him, and that Biddy could do not good for him. If it were a 'blast' from the fairies (a fairy wind) Biddy would be able to cure him.[41]

Biddy preferred not to get money, and she often said so, gifts in kind were more acceptable to her. This was in keeping with the old Irish tradition as it was believed that if the healer demanded payment, their powers would be taken away from them.

A woman who lived in Quinn, Co. Clare, had been ill for some time and was not improving, so it was suggested that somebody should seek Biddy Early's aid. The story is told by a man from Six-milebridge.

My grandfather, Martin Fahy of Quinn, went to Biddy Early for this woman. He travelled by gennet and car. When he arrived at Tulla village he went into a public house and had a few drinks. On his way from there to Kilbarron, he went astray. He met a woman on the road and he asked her for directions. But he later discovered that she put him on the wrong road, and it took him a long time to reach Biddy's.

When he did arrive Biddy said, 'Come in,' and to his surprise told him everything that had happened since he left home at an early hour that morning. She told him that he could be at her house two hours before the time he arrived, only for the woman putting him astray on the road. She warned him as she gave him a little bottle, that it would be taken from him unless he kept a good grip of it, and to be extra careful at a certain spot in Tulla.

On coming to this spot near Tulla, the gennet stood and started to shiver. Martin had the bottle in the inside pocket of his overcoat, and when he saw the gennet frightened, he gripped it tightly. Then a terrible struggle took place for the bottle, by invisible people, but Martin, fighting hard, held on to the bottle. At this time the gennet was moving over a little stream which was flowing under the road.

Martin arrived at the sick woman's house about twelve o'clock that night. With Biddy's instructions the contents of the bottle were sprinkled on the woman. Next morning she came from her bed in her usual good health.[42]

Margaret Murphy, now in her eighties, lives a short distance from Biddy Early's cottage and tells the following story.

My grandmother had a sister married, and she got very, very ill, and the doctor pronounced she had fever and that no one was to go to the house, and my grandmother used to go to the window and talk in to her. And she said to her that she didn't think she had the fever, and said, 'Would you go to Biddy Early for me?'

'I will,' says my grandmother, and she walked all the way from Cahirhurley, outside Bodyke, to Biddy.

'She has not fever,' said Biddy. 'I'm giving you a bottle now, but you'll be a brave woman if you'll carry it back safely. You'll have to hold on tight to it.'

'The dickins will be in it,' my grandmother said, 'I'll hold it.' So she did. And she hadn't come very far beyond Fitz's well, when she was jostled and tossed around the road, but she held on to her bottle, and when she went down to Ballinahinch cross, she got another tossing there, but she held on to the bottle, and gave it to her sister. Next morning, the sister was up doing her work.

My father used to play cards at Biddy's with the lads around, sure it was only over the road from here, and people used to go on *cuairds* to her house the same as they would to anybody else's house. But of course there was a great attraction towards Biddy's, as she always had plenty drink, in fact she had too much of it and made many of the lads fond of it. People who came for cures brought presents; but whiskey, a jar of whiskey, was a favourite present. And another thing, the priests discouraged people from having too much to do with her, some spoke out strongly against her. Of course this place was thickly populated at the time.

She was really Mrs Flannery at that time. But I remember my father telling me about one night they were in her house playing cards, and there was no such thing as playing for money that time, they'd play for drink. Anyway the party who won was pressing the loosers to go into the village and get the drink. Biddy said, 'Take your time, we'll soon have enough of it.' It wasn't coming anyway, and the winners were getting very impatient, and were pressing the other boys to go to Feakle. And then Biddy went out, and she came in saying, 'Sit down now, there's plenty of it coming up at Ballinahinch Cross.' And my father said that shortly after, a horse and car pulled into the yard outside, and there was a girl inside in it, tied down with ropes she was. Seemingly she had suddenly gone mental and was very bad. Biddy was talking and saying things to her, and she cured her after a while. Then they danced until morning. There was a blind fiddler around here, Paddy Mac, and he played for them. And my father said, that the girl was the finest step dancer he ever saw on any floor.

There was always plenty of food in the house, because people were always bringing items like batches of bread, flour, home-made butter, as well as the drink.[43]

CHAPTER NINE

Curing and foretelling together with drinking and card-playing did not find favour with the local Catholic clergy, who openly spoke out against the deeds and words of Biddy Early. Her 'magic' cures were treated by them with great suspicion, many believing that her power was obtained from evil sources — 'The Devil' they said. She had, therefore, several heated confrontations with the priests.

'All dealings and communications with the devil; and inquiring by improper means after things which are lost, hidden, or to come,' was the code which the Catholic Church expressed.

To the priests who heard of Biddy Early's deeds, she was violating that code, in part at least; her actions indicated that she was working against the law of God. The future was said to be in God's hands, and was not meant to be questioned in any way.

Continuous efforts were made by the Church to erase beliefs in superstitious practices, and the clergy were constantly being encouraged by their bishops to speak out against these survivals of paganism.

In the seventh century one of the homilies delivered by St Eloi in France said: 'If any sickness should attack you, have recourse neither to enchanters, nor to soothsayers, nor to engravers of amulets. Having nothing to do with wells, trees, or cross-roads, with the object of performing charms, but let him who is sick have confidence in the mercy of God alone.'

Locally, the writings of an Englishman, William West were quoted: 'An enchanter or charmer was recognised... by certain words spoken, and characters or images, herbs or other things applied, [they] think they can do anything they like, the devil so deceives them, or by his action does those things which the enchanters would have done...'

Because such words were being preached, it was difficult for the peasants of rural Ireland to understand whether the power that an individual like Biddy Early had came from a demon or from God. Naturally many feared her and would have nothing to do with her.[44]

I knew a man named Tom Hayes that lived in Barr A Geagaim about seventy years ago. Tom told the local parish priest in confession that he went to Biddy for a cure. The priest told him that as a penance he'd have to go bare-headed and bare-footed, and show himself to Father Bowler P.P. of Tulla. He had to do it. [Pat MacNamara].[45]

My uncle Jim Minogue lived near Biddy at Kilbarron. He got a fever. People were forbidden by the Church to go to Biddy. So my grandmother would not allow Jim to be brought to her. Jim got better again. Next day after that, my mother and Biddy were beating clothes in a little stream. 'Your mother would not let Jim come near me. Jim is better now. Your mother will come to see me next time,' she said. The next time he got bad, he died.[46]

51

The rumour had spread that she had been ex-communicated, as Biddy had given up the outward practice of her religion and was not seen attending Feakle Mass on Sundays. There is no evidence that this was true; a possible explanation is that she refused to sit in the congregation and be insulted from the altar.

When the priest roared from the pulpit to beware of those who take God's law into their own hands, and when he struck the timber with his fist, warning his fellow brethren not to show strangers where Biddy lived,[47] they listened; they feared 'the Witch' amongst them. Also they believed the power of the priest was great, and they dreaded the warning they were getting about hell's fire.

I was with Biddy Early myself one time, and got a cure from her for my little girl that was sick. A bottle of whiskey I brought her, and the first thing she did was to open it, and to give me a glass out of it. 'For,' says she, 'you'll maybe want it my poor man.' But I had plenty courage in those days. The priests were against her; often Father Boyle would speak of her in his sermons. They can all do those cures themselves, but that's a thing it's not right to be talking about.[48]

There was a neighbour of my own, Andrew Dennehy: I was knocked up by him one night to go to the house, because he said *They* [the fairies] were calling to him. But when [we] got there, there was nothing to be found. But some see these things, and some can't. It's against our creed to believe in them. And the priests won't let on that they believe in them themselves, but they are more in dread of going about at night than any of us. They were against Biddy Early too. There was a man I knew living near the sea, and he set out to go to her one time. And on his way he went into his brother-in-law's house, and the priest came in there, and bid him not to go on. 'Well, Father,' says he, 'cure me yourself if you won't let me go to her to be cured.' And when the priest wouldn't do that (for the priests can do many cures if they like to) he went on to her. And the minute he came in, 'well,' says she, 'you made a great fight for me on the way.' For thought it's against our creed to believe it, she could hear any earthly thing that was said in every part, miles off.[49]

In spite of all the condemnation, she defied the Church and all its powers and against it she courageously and successfully used her own personal powers. Dermot MacManus has written:

These weapons were the undoubted cures which she effected, for while she would and did cure people and animals, as well as crops, the parish priest could not; nor could the bishop, nor any other member of the Irish hierarchy. Clearly, this was the acid test. When people urgently wanted themselves or the dear ones or their animals to be saved, it was to Biddy they turned, knowing that she alone could do so if she wished. Nothing that the parish priest might say or do could prevent them from going to her, even if only clandestinely, in the total absence of any alternative cure by the Church.[50]

On one occasion the parish priest of Quinn and his curate were living together in the parish priest's residence of Willpark, Quinn. This was before the curate's house was built in the village of Quinn. Their housekeeper was the parish priest's niece, Mary O'Dwyer. Fr McMahon, the curate, had a craze for hunting, and he always kept a horse and two dogs for the purpose. Himself and the housekeeper were constantly quarreling, because he was always late for meals, and this was the cause of unnecessary trouble for the housekeeper. One day he was late coming in to his dinner, and he said something to her. She insulted him, and he gave her a tap of his whip on the leg. Later in the day the leg began to pain. Some suggested Biddy Early. Next day while out hunting Fr McMahon told Martin Fahy, and Martin suggested taking her to Biddy. But the priest wouldn't agree. So Martin suggested he would do so himself, and he took her next day.

Biddy was at the door waiting. 'I see you have brought the priest's niece for me to heal her swollen leg,' says she. 'He doesn't deserve to have it cured, but for her own sake I will cure it. Come in yourself, but don't bring in the girl.' She gave Martin a meal, and when he had it finished she gave him a drop of whiskey for the road. Then she put a drop of something in the bottle, and gave it to Martin to give to the priest. 'Tell him to cure her himself, because he was the cause of the injury.'

When they arrived back at Wellpark, Fr McMahon wasn't at home, so Martin went away without seeing him, but he took care to leave the bottle with Biddy's instructions, at the house. The girl was cured alright, but she had a lame step for the rest of her life.[51]

If you went to confession, the priest wouldn't give you absolution if you had talked to Biddy Early. 'Twas all saddle horses were in those days, there were no motor cars or anything. 'Myself I remember when there was no bicycle, the first bicycle was a three-hapenny bicycle, a big wheel and a small wheel, I saw a lad riding off along the road here, and we were following him wondering what he was riding. But anyway, this priest from Tipperary... 'Twas all horses and saddles the curate had that time. But this curate came on from Tipperary, he came on in to Fr Mee, in Feakle, he was the parish priest. 'And where here above does Biddy Early live?' says he to the parish priest.

'About a mile,' says he.

He got up on the saddle and off he went down the road. He tied the horse at the end of the avenue and went up as far as Biddy. She was in the yard. He saluted her. 'Are you the woman they call Biddy Early?' says he.

'Well, they call me that anyway, Father,' says she.

'Well, you wrath of a devil, what's keeping you here, bringing misfortune down on the parish,' says he, 'with your devilment and your cursing and your pishogues. If you don't lave this,' says he, 'and stop that, I'll put you into the lake below in a ball of fire.'

'Ye're great men, wonderful great men,' says Biddy.

He went all round the room with his whip, cracking the lash around the room to knock fright out of Biddy. He walked away, he walked down the avenue, and he turned back. 'If I come back again to see you, you'll remember me.'

'You'll remember me too,' says she, 'before you're gone very far.'

He was very vexed, he went down, gave no heed to Biddy. He went up on the saddle, pulled his horse, and he stepped away about a quarter of a mile, and at a place called Annasala Bridge, the horse stood up on the road, and he drew the whip. And when he went to draw the whip, his hand would make no hand to shove for the whip. When he went to bring his legs off the saddle his legs wouldn't come out of the stirrup. So he couldn't come off 'a the saddle, nor his horse wouldn't go.

There he was, and he from Tipperary. . . and no go, no go at all.

'Gor,' says he, 'I'm done.'

Then there did a little man come down the road walking, he called him over. 'Come over,' says he, 'I want you. Do you know Biddy Early here?' says he.

'Oh, I do, Father, I know her well.'

'What kind is she?'

'Oh, a fine honest woman.'

'Would you go down,' says he. 'Would you go in to her and ask her. Tell her there's a priest above in the road, and he can't come off 'a the saddle, nor his horse won't walk. And don't let me here all night, and ask her for God's sake, and I'll never again bother her, or I'll never again say a word to her. Sure she might be righter than what we are.'

By gor, the man went in to Biddy. 'Biddy,' says he, 'there's a priest above in the road and his horse won't walk, he can't come off 'a the

56

saddle, nor he can't strike the horse. He told me
to go in to you, and for God's sake to let him go
home, and he'll never bother you again. He says
you're honester than the people themselves that
brought him.'

'Ah, he was a great bully here a few minutes
ago, a great bully. But I'll tell you 'tis easy to
quieten those bullys. And I'll quieten 'um,' says
she.

'Let the poor man go, Biddy. Leave him go
this time.'

'I will,' says she, 'I'll forgive him this time. Go
over to that white-thorn bush beyond over-right
the door and bring me hither three thraneens,'
says she. And he brought them hither; and
Biddy went up to her room; then she came
down. 'Here now, give them to him, and tell him
strike his horse on the right shoulder, in the
name of the Father, and of the Son and of the
Holy Ghost. And tell that priest when he's at
home, to mind his own business, and not to
mind me.'

'Oh, then that's what I'll do,' says he. Off he
went, and he gave the tree thraneens to the
priest, and the priest struck the horse on the
right shoulder 'In the name of the Father, and of
the Son and of the Holy Ghost.'

'Well, the horse struck his hind legs against
the road, and out with him, past Hayes' forge,
and up the Barrick Line. . . And faith he never
returned to Feakle or Biddy Early any more.
[Nevilles Horan] [52]

A similar event occurred some years later:

A man on his way to Feakle fair was passing

Biddy's house, he called in to light his pipe and she bade him be seated as usual. He sat down, and they began to discuss various topics, and during the conversation the man himself drew down about the 'black art'. When he said this, Biddy said to him, 'I suppose you drew down this because you hear people talking about me, and they say that I am working in the power of the devil. But I tell you that I am not, my power comes from 'the good people' who are rightly named Good. It's the priests are the cause of my unpopularity with many people. But wait, I will change their tune very soon.[53]

The man continued on his journey, but he remembered this when he heard what happened to the parish priest.

The parish priest of Feakle, who had not succeeded in keeping his parishioners away from Biddy, decided he would face this imposter in person. So he saddled his horse and rode out in the afternoon. Having tied the animal to a bush at the end of the boreen, he walked angrily up to the cottage. Arriving at the half-door, he hardly waited to knock, but stormed in to Biddy, who was seated in a chair beside the hearth.

Neither surprised nor annoyed, she greeted him, *'Failte romhait'*.

'By the time you've heard what I have to say, you won't be pleased that I called,' he snapped, and he continued to tell her what he thought of her behaviour and the spirits she was invoking. Finally he set before her a picture of what the next world would be like for her if she did not mend her ways.

Quite composed, she listened. When he stopped, she spoke out vigorously to him, and told him in no uncertain terms that she was doing her own business and that he should let her in peace.

Giving her a final warning, he stamped out the door. 'Be careful on the way home, Father,' she called after him.

Down he went, untied his horse, jumped up on him, but there was no way in which he could get the animal to move. Full of anger after his encounter with Biddy, he beat him, and told him to get going. But it was all in vain. In desperation after repeated blows, the horse reared, and threw his rider heavily to the ground.

When he regained composure, a little shaken, he walked over to the horse, patted and soothed it for a few moments, and tried to encourage the horse to walk forward. But the animal refused to take even one step. Eventually, after much effort, the priest was forced to give up the struggle and had to return to Biddy.

She admitted she had prevented the horse from moving, and apologising for the inconvenience, she told him that the spell would be lifted when he got back, and that he could ride home without further trouble.

When the priest returned to his horse, he found that Biddy had been true to her word. He returned home; and though he did not speak out against her after that, neither did he lavish any praise on her.[54]

Being a forceful person, she was not intimidated by anybody and always took a firm line, respecting the clergy only in so far as they showed themselves deserving of respect.

A priest went to her one time in plain clothes in

order to find out her secrets. Biddy recognised him at once. 'There is nothing wrong with you, Father,' says she, 'but you are coming to find out my secrets.'

'You can go again as you came,' says she.[55]

CHAPTER TEN

Tom Flannery worked mainly as a labourer. He had 'thrown up' the cabin at Kilbarron shortly before he married Biddy, having paid a certain number of days' work for a patch of ground. By paying in labour and in money after the crop was harvested, he was able to obtain conacre ground. It was a gamble, but was the method in which the poorest Irish depended. If the season was good, it sometimes meant a profit, if it was bad, it meant ruination.

The Penal Laws in Ireland dated from 1695 and meant that Catholics were debarred from important offices in the country, and these laws were not repealed until the Catholic Emancipation Act of 1829. During and after this time the Catholic peasants bore the full brunt of the hardships: high rent without fixed tenancy, living in cabins well warmed with a natural turf fire but ill-clothed and often sleeping on a bed of hay or straw on a mud floor.

Most landlords cared little about what went on on the estates, their main interest being the maximum income. The tenants under such bosses could not hope to receive any help, nor to reap the benefits of their own improvements.

By 1845, the majority of the Irish peasants were dependant on the land which was divided and subdivided due to an increase in population. Some had only a few acres and indeed many had less. Unless

61

an Irish labourer had a patch on which to grow potatoes to feed himself and his family, they would starve.

Potatoes, commonly called spuds, were the staple diet of the people, so there was much hardship when there was a partial crop failure in 1845. Evicted families wandered about begging, and many, wasted by disease and hardship, lived and died in the fields and by the roadsides.

As in all the households in the district the Flannery home was invaded by poverty. Biddy would not take anything from those who could not afford it and helped any who sought her aid, in so far as this was possible. Tenure payments were a burden which she and her husband had to face, and during the years which followed they lost part of the holding. Nevertheless, they managed to keep their mud cabin and to survive in the midst of mass starvation.

Mainly to keep the Irish poor from invading England, an Irish Poor Law Act had been passed in 1838 which provided for Relief Workhouses throughout the country. In Ennis, in 1841, a workhouse was built to accommodate the poor of the district.[56] Only those who were absolutely destitute were admitted. During the famine years, disease and fever were rampant and so the majority who were admitted died within its walls.

Biddy was only too well aware of the hardship and degradation which accompanied life in a workhouse, so she helped many of the neighbours to gather herbs and berries which they could cook in order to survive.

The year 1847 became known as the Black '47 when, following a foggy, wet June and July, blight once more hit the potatoes. Many died the horrible death of starvation or from the accompanying fever. The population in the district of Feakle was by the end of this period reduced by more than half, and there were many mass-burials in fields. In later years Biddy was able to sense these locations, and advised the people not to touch them.

Towards the end of these difficult years a personal tragedy struck Biddy. The story is told of a man who had asked a priest to cure his only child who was dying. When the priest was unable to do so, the man went to Biddy and said, 'I know you can cure him.'

'I can cure him alright, but it will be costly on me.'

And it is alleged that she cured the child, but her own son died.

Was it a transference of misfortune? Would her son have died in any case? What ever went on in the heart of this Irish mother who lost her only son, nobody ever knew; she kept it all within.

CHAPTER ELEVEN

After the famine, although now over fifty years old, Biddy was still youthful looking with a fresh complexion and no noticeable grey hairs. Nature's herbs, fresh butter, milk and eggs were perhaps contributing factors. During her trips outside the house she covered her head with a white linen bonnet, the frills of which outlined her face.

Her reputation never stopped growing. Stories of her were on the lips of the travelling tin-smith and the travelling cobbler as they journeyed from house to house and the title of 'Witch' was now the one most commonly used. Her ability was a combination of a spirit-given healing within her magnetic hands, intelligence and a dash of traditional lore.

She used her bottle as a clairvoyant would use a crystal ball, gazing into it to discover what she needed to know and acting accordingly. Word circulated that there was a little coffin inside and that if it lay flat, the person would die; if it stood on edge, the patient would be cured. That Biddy had a power beyond the capacity of most individuals was something which the people could not easily dismiss and they were firm in the belief that the spirits or the fairies were her guiding factor.

In rural Ireland, horses were very precious. They were required to plough and till the fields, and were the only means of transportation, so that if a horse got sick, his owner was concerned for the livelihood of the family.

Biddy is reputed to have cured many an animal, but very often, though not always, her power in curing meant the transference of the sickness to some other living creature.

There was a man in Ballycar who owned a valuable stallion. When the man arose one morning his servant told him that the stallion was sick. The man went immediately to the stable and found the horse was unable to move. He brought a veterinary surgeon and he could do nothing for the stallion. The man was advised by some of his neighbours to go to Biddy Early. He went and told her about the stallion. She said she could not cure the horse without putting the illness on something else. He agreed. Then Biddy looked into her famous bottle and told the man that when he would go home his stallion would be cured.

When he went home his stallion was cured, but his servant boy was ill and his face was twisted. So the man went again to Biddy Early, telling her what had happened. She took the evil off the servant boy and put it on the horse once more. When the man went home the horse was dead.[57]

This transference could also, however, work in the opposite direction.

There was a couple from Leitrim, who were not long married. They were returning home from Loughrea on horseback when the horse shied, and the young man was thrown off and he was injured. He got very ill, and his young wife seeing him, sent immediately for the doctor, and he gave him medical assistance. The poor woman was afraid, because if anything happened a husband shortly after getting married, then the wife would have to go home to her own people, that was the rule of the time.

Fearing the worst, she got a loan of an ass and cart, and set out for Biddy Early. After telling the story, Biddy gave her a small bottle, and bade her protect it on the way home.

'Sprinkle a drop on your husband, and make the sign of the cross, in the name of the Father and of the Son and of the Holy Ghost,' she said. Then she praised the land around Kilcooley castle,

And when the woman was leaving Biddy said, 'Tell your husband to come to see me when he's better.'

It was not long until he was as right as rain, and off he set for Biddy's house. He chatted with her for a while, and when he was returning home, didn't the horse shy in the very same spot, but this time, the young fellow was on his own, and he held tight. But next morning, what happened when he went into the stable? Wasn't the horse dead. So isn't it plain to be seen that Biddy cared for the man, and took the horse instead.[58]

It was extremely unwise not to follow Biddy's instructions to the letter.

This is a true story. There was a family who lived near Rosscaure Chapel. He was an R.I.C. sergeant They had an only daughter who got delicate. Friends advised her to take her to Biddy Early. So the mother took them to Biddy who gave her a bottle of medicine and told her to come back to her that day seven years. The girl went home, and as the days past she got well, and grew up over the years into a fine strong young woman. All the neighbours wondered very much at the remarkable recovery. My grandmother was a great friend of this girl's mother. One evening when returning from Woodford she called in to see her. They spoke about the wonderful change in the daughter's health and remarked what a fine woman she grew to be. Then the mother of the young woman recalled that the following day was the date fixed by Biddy Early for the return visit of the young woman. She however said they would not bother going. They laughed at the thought of the return visit. Next morning, both mother and daughter were found dead. There was no question of poison, or foul play. [Kathleen Donellan] [59]

CHAPTER TWELVE

Like most areas in the country, Feakle, Biddy Early's home parish, was not without its secret societies. Since the Irish peasant felt that the law did not give him justice, he often took it into his own hands. Secret societies became widespread during the Penal period and continued in a succession of underground associations — Oak Boys, White Boys, Ribbon Men and Moonlighters. They met in bogs and glens and dispensed rough justice in revenge for evictions and the hanging of peasants for misdemeanours. The aim was to eliminate strong-willed landlords.

During the late 1850s and 1860s the Clare Moonlighters were in full swing and one of them, a relation of Biddy's nicknamed 'Mick the Moonlighter', was very prominent in the struggle. He held twenty acres as a tenant and lived in a mud cabin on this holding. Apparently the landlord (who was a brother of Sheehy who had evicted Biddy, and suffered for the deed, many years before) learned of his involvement in this secret society, and consequently gave him notice to leave within eighteen days. This he refused to do. A second notice came and he refused this also, as he was paying his rent. As anticipated, the dreaded 'crow-bar gang' arrived one afternoon. Mick and many of his friends from hamlets close by fought a tough battle, but eventually they were forced to surrender, and Mick's home was razed to the ground.

Mick decided to get his revenge. One night he set out for the landlord's house. Quietly he stole towards it and was able to view the well-lit sitting room through an opening in the curtains. In one end the landlord's wife stood with her hands around her daughter, and at the far corner sat the fifty-year-old man stooped over a book.

Mick was ready to pull the trigger when a hand was laid on his shoulder. It was McCaw, one of the servants. As the two tussled, the door opened and the boss emerged, whereupon Mick fired two volleys at him and ran as quickly as he could into the darkness.

He spent part of that night in a secluded cabin among the moors, but the next night, a close friend of his having died, he felt he should go to the wake, so off he went cross-country to the house. In the lower room where a group of women were chatting around a turf fire, he overheard them tell of how the landlord, Alderman Sheehy, had been murdered the previous night. As Mick made his way to the room where the body was waked, somebody gave the alarm, "The Peelers are abroad.'

Mick had a second reason for coming to the wake; his girl friend was a sister of the dead man. Quickly he acted; he called her, whispered something into her ear and shortly after emerged in a dress and hat and knelt beside the women mourners.

In a fury the police came into the house. They entered the wake room. Looking around and seeing no man, they expressed apologies for their intrusion, paid their respects to the dead, and quietly withdrew from the room and left the house.

Mick soon learned that they were considering

placing a reward, dead or alive, on his head, for 'murdering a loyal subject of His Majesty'. He knew that his only salvation lay in his cousin Biddy, as she had got him out of trouble before over his 'moonlighting'.

As he hurried along across the hills and dells and bogs, he glanced around now and then to assure himself that he was not seen or followed by the police.

The church bells of Feakle were chiming the noon-day Angelus and filled his ears with the music of Heaven when Mick, weary and tired, arrived at the witch's home. She was dining quietly by herself at a small table set back in the corner of the kitchen, which was spacious and remarkably clean and tidy. She welcomed him and invited him to partake of a cup of tea which he did, as he felt quite hungry after his journey. Overhead the table on the wall hung a huge, magnificent picture depicting Napoleon and his triumphal march across Europe. Mick, who had read a great deal about this immortal French warrior, made a reference to it and Biddy said that Napoleon would never have got so far as he did but for the advice and instruction he had got from the Queen of Magic, and that, but for he had fallen out with her, he would have defeated England at Waterloo, and would have ruled the world.

'Who was the Queen of Magic?' asked Mick.

'She lived near Paris in them times, and was the writer of that book,' replied Biddy, pointing her finger at a book which lay on a shelf over the mantlepiece. It was an immense volume, about nine inches thick, and bore the title: *My Rambles Through Fairyland.*

The tea over, Mick, without further delay, related his tale of woe to Biddy, who was a medium-sized woman with a broad countenance ornamented with an aquiline nose, and two diamond like eyes which seemed to be looking miles and miles away, listened attentively.[60]

'I didn't mean to kill him, Biddy, honest, I didn't. I only wanted to injure him. Give him a taste of his own medicine. The killing was an accident,' he said.

'I know that, I know that,' she replied.

Mick, fearing the dreaded death by hanging, said to her.

'Tell me, please tell me what to do.' Whereupon she rose and got her dark 'magic' bottle. After a short interval of concentration, she advised him that his only means of escape was to go to the village of Liscannor.

'There you will find a fishing trawler anchored. Your escape will be by sea to Kilrush, and from there to America.'

Mick, making towards the door, paused for a moment, 'How will I avoid the Peelers?'

'You won't meet the Peelers,' Biddy said, and looking into her bottle once more, she continued, 'Avoid the towns, Ennis and Ennistymon. And go now.'

Before leaving, he told Biddy to advise his girlfriend what to do. 'Let her follow me and find me. You'll know what course she should take.'[61]

Some hours after 'Mick the Moonlighter' had left Biddy, the police came to her house and arrested her husband as an accessary to the crime. They

71

had been informed of Mick's call, and were also aware where the sympathies of Biddy and Tom Flannery lay. As with all secret societies, there were informers who were well rewarded for giving information. Also they knew that Biddy could help them in their search, if she wished.

According to a newspaper report on 13 November 1860, six men were lodged in Ennis Gaol on suspicion of having been implicated in the death of Alderman Sheehy near Feakle. They were escorted to jail by the Tulla police; and the report also states that one of the men was Flannery, the husband of 'the witch' Biddy Early. Other names given were Minogue, Burke, and another Flannery known as 'whiskers'.[62]

On Tuesday morning, 13 November 1860, a meeting was convened in the Grand Jury Room of the Ennis Courthouse by the Right Hon. Lord Inchiquin, Lieutenant and *Custos Rotulorum* of Clare, to enquire into the circumstances surrounding the murder of Alderman William Sheehy. The meeting was held behind closed doors and the press was excluded. Lord Inchiquin was in the chair for this important meeting, which brought many well-known magistrates from all corners of Ireland.[63]

Following the meeting, a public announcement was made.

We the undersigned magistrates subscribe the sum placed opposite our respective names, for such information as shall lead to the apprehension and conviction of any of the persons engaged in the murder of Mr William Sheehy, at Ayle, on the 23rd, October, 1860, within twelve months from the date hereof; one fourth of the said sum will be given for such private information as shall lead to the conviction of any of the parties concerned in the murder.

The amount subscribed was £150.[64]

Any men who had an involvement with 'The Moonlighters' were immediately suspicious characters.

A newspaper report on 16 December 1860[65] states that Martin Minogue, arrested on suspicion of the murder of Alderman Sheehy, was on the previous day fully committed for trial. The depositions were read over him in Ennis Gaol, he having been brought from Tulla Bridewell where he had been in custody for the previous week. It was here also that testimony of the principal witness had been taken.

According to the report, 'Flannery, the husband of Biddy Early, the "witch" was also in Ennis Goal yesterday.' He too heard the depositions read over him and was charged with alleged participation in the crime. It stated that bail would probably be taken at the next Assizes, as his part in the crime was allegedly not as great as that of Minogue.

Mr O'Hara, who was the Resident Magistrate read the depositions in 'the Gaol Office', the two prisoners having been brought from the interior of the prison for that purpose. Mr Cullinan, their solicitor, was present and had advised the men not to speak during the proceedings. At the next Assizes, bail money was lodged and Flannery and Minogue were released.

According to further newspaper reports, the case against them was dropped. Apparently it was learned that the man solely responsible for the killing could not be caught, as he had left the country. A play based on this incident was later written and published by Patrick Dollard.[66]

Joy filled Biddy's heart when a year later she received a letter from Mick, who had settled in America, containing instructions for his girlfriend to follow.[67]

CHAPTER THIRTEEN

My father used to tell me that there was always lines of asses and carts, all along the road there. They came from all over. She cured so many, and told them where to find animals. And she would also remove a 'bad-spell' cast by the evil eye on a person. [Margaret Murphy] [68]

She was taken to a girl outside Bodyke for each of three days, because 'Red Haired Moll' cast an 'evil eye' on the girl. She was said to have been possessed with an evil spirit, but Biddy eventually restored her to normality. [69]

Hundreds of years of tradition had gone into every twist and turn connected with the dairy. So much depended on the butter — the rent, the wages, money for most things, in fact the difference between plenty and want. There was only a thin dividing line between the two in most farmers' holdings, so much so that everything connected with the cows, the milking and the churning was treated with a sort of sacredness — even down to the very spancels. These, used for tying the cows legs to keep them quiet during milking time, were made from the hair cut from the cows tails around April or May and wound into ropes; they were carefully guarded for if a neighbour took a spancel, he could take the year's milk.

Many superstitions were woven around the

making of butter. The milk was usually set in large earthenware pans, while daily the top cream was skimmed off, put into other containers until churning day. If days had been spent without getting it 'to turn' then an evil spell had been cast. Continually Biddy was being called on to remove the spell, so that the butter could be restored to the injured party.

There was a man living in a townland and known as Lissycasey. He was a well-to-do farmer and had a great number of cows. He used to make a good deal of butter every week. One May Eve, he went churning and he was churning for hours and hours, but he did not succeed in making any butter, so he ceased churning. Every week from May Eve to July he failed to make butter. He suspected there was some person doing him evil, so he decided on going to Biddy Early to consult her. He went and as he was entering the house she met him at the door, and before he could say one word she said, 'I know what brought you here, and the person that is taking the butter from you is supposed to be a dear friend of yours, but behind your back he is your enemy, and at present he has a calf sick, and the calf will die in two days' time.' She told him also to watch where his neighbour will bury the calf, and she said, 'he will bury the calf between the hours of twelve and one o'clock at night.'

The man returned home and watched as Biddy had told him. He saw his neighbour bringing the dead calf and burying it in his land. He did not mention it to any person but went to Biddy Early next morning. When she saw him, she told him all that had happened him since he left before. She also told him that it was not the first animal his neighbour had buried in his land, that he had a number of them buried there. She said, 'Go back and ask him to dig up all the animals he has buried on your land.' She also gave him a bottle, and told him to shake the contents of it where the animals would be dug up. So the man returned home, and with a good deal of arguing he got his neighbour to do as Biddy Early had said. And when everything was fixed, all the butter that had gone from the man for the past three months came back gradually to him, and the other man had never much luck afterwards.[70]

I used to see people visiting her in order that she might hold the year's butter for them. This was from May to May. They would always visit her on May Day, the day on which the butter would be taken. Every day for the whole month of April, I used to see the West Clare people passing on their way to Biddy. [Jim Fitzgerald][71]

Throughout her life, she was extremely successful in finding cattle. If any were lost or stolen in County Clare or any of the surrounding counties, the pass-word was, 'Biddy will find them with her magic bottle.'

My grandmother was a Shea woman from County Limerick. She got a present of two calves when she was a young girl, and one fine morning they disappeared off the lands. Her brother consulted Biddy Early about her loss, and Biddy said, 'The people who are coming every morning to the house sympathising with you on the loss of your calves are the people who carried away your cattle. They are going by boat today from

Limerick. Hurry on or they will be gone.' They rushed back to Limerick and went to the boat where they found the missing cattle.[72]

On another occasion her help was sought by two brothers whose cattle had strayed from home. She told them where they were, but remarked, 'You'd be better off if they were never found.' When the boys arrived home with the cattle, an argument arose between them as to who was the lawful owner of the stock. And in the heated blows which followed, one of the brothers was killed.[73]

This is true, it has to do with my wife's family in Graigue. One of the older neighbours there missed a bullock — a yearling. As his stock consisted of three or four cows with their calves, and would mean a grievous cross to the poor man. After a while, as there was no trace of the calf, so he was advised to try 'The Wise Woman of Clare.'

Before setting out he went into the forge there at the cross and had a few words with the smith. Coming away, said he, 'I know I'm a fool to be going.' The smith was a young man who placed hardly any faith in old nonsense like that, although his father was supposed to have got sure information upon a problem troubling him, from Biddy Early, several years before that.

When he landed in Clare at Biddy's house, she greeted him with, 'So this is the fool from Graigue who is afraid that Biddy Early won't find his old bullock. She won't find it, but you will get it all the same when a red-haired man will come into your yard.' He was offering her money, but she would not take any as she said, 'You need it much more than I do. And tell that lad of a smith to go lighter with his hammer, or

78

he'll burn his puss one of these days. He's a bit of a joker, but that'll teach him to be civil,' she said.

The smith was a joker, but what smith wasn't? And sure enough in the cutting of a piece from a bar of red hot iron some time after that, the piece, through some awkwardness of the striker, jumped and burned the smith's lip.

As regards the bullock, in a few days in walked a red-haired man who worked away as a boy, with one of the farmers in Kilmallock. On his way home to Graigue, he happened to pass through an outside farm where the farmer had some dry stock, and here he noticed the strange bullock, and upon enquiries he found out who the owner was.[74]

She [Biddy] was brought here to Cahirburley on a horse. Someone was sick, and there is a house, or was a house below there. But when she came to the cross, she said, 'Who's living in there?' There was a new house after being put up, 'twas thatched of course, but they all were that time.

'Tady Walsh,' she was told.

'Oh,' she said, 'that can't be there, that's in a path.'

'But,' she was told, 'that's a new house.'

'I don't mind,' she said, 'that's in a path. That can't be there long.'

Well, I heard that when I was a young lad, and I wasn't very old when the house went, that you wouldn't know what 'twas. The house was knocked, and there was a road made there. But 'twas an awful wonder at the time, because 'twas a fine big thatched house. But we were able to trace a row of whitethorns running south-east from the house. The whitethorns were the mark of a fairy path. [Sonny Walsh] [75]

Sonny Walsh continues:

And I know a little field here, and the people who owned it often went to her about something. But she told them never to till that field that's at the eastern side of the house. Well I never walk around it, that I don't think of Biddy and the hollow. A brother-in-law of mine did plough it, not the hollow but the field. One of the horses went into the hollow, the year after the horse died. Then we thought of the hollow, it's a strange kind of a sunken patch in the field. Those coincidences can't be stretched very far in lots of cases. It's strange. But you know, deep down in all of us, there is something which makes us wonder. [76]

CHAPTER FOURTEEN

Life with Tom Flannery was pleasant for Biddy. He was a carefree man, popular with the lads, young, gay and always willing to join in the activities of the moment. There was never a dull moment in the Flannery home; throughout the day, callers frequented the cabin and at night it was a great house to go on *cuaird*, with card-playing, step-dancing and singing and whiskey was plentiful with its companion poteen.

Just over a year later in 1865 she was to appear before the court in Ennis. Under the 1586 Statute, she was charged with taking part in witchcraft.

The police had found her a nuisance, as she helped those whom 'the law' would like to have out of the way. Also they knew she kept illegal spirits in the house, yet persistent raids proved fruitless. Her actions were also being brought into question by a Limerick doctor as well as the Catholic clergy.

My grandfather was a local Grand-Jurer here at the time, [says Cormac Halpin]. And he defended her when she appeared before the court on a charge of medling in Witchcraft.[77]

Confident, Biddy, dressed in her home-spuns and frilly white bonnet was brought to court in a horse and cart driven by her husband.

But when the case opened, many of those who had said they would give evidence against her took fright and kept silent. So, triumphantly, Biddy won the day. The case was dismissed, 'due to lack of sufficient evidence against the accused.'

In 1868, another personal tragedy hit Biddy. Her husband Tom got sick and after a short illness, he died at home in the cabin on 25 June. And though Dr McDonagh attended him, he refused to give a certificate. A neighbour, Pat Meany, was also present at the time of his death.[78]

He was waked in the little room where all the neighbours came to pay their respects, and later he was buried in a plot in Feakle graveyard.

She always felt sad when alone, especially during the night because by day she was seldom without company. During the hours of darkness, she was left with the memories of the early loss of her parents, three dead husbands and a dead son.

CHAPTER FIFTEEN

There never yet was a man who had fifty thousand pounds that hadn't more wants than any beggar-man going from door to door.

Your mind, not your money, that makes you rich. Contentment is a blessing a millionaire's wealth couldn't purchase. If you would make a man happy, do not add to his possessions, but subtract from the sum of his desires. The less you desire the happier you are, and, the happier you are, the richer you are. That's what I believe, and that's why I have no value for money.[79]

So said Biddy Early when told she would get a ransom for informing on one of her fellow peasants.

She never rose above the poverty line, but according to herself she had mental riches that money couldn't buy. 'My gift, such as it is, is a purely natural gift. It was born with me; it is a part of me, like the hair on my head. . . '[80]

Many a caller received a welcome cup of tea from her, and she sometimes gave the children a slice of bread when she discovered them peeping in the window at her as they strolled home from school.

She never took money, but was given gifts of flour and meal as well as other items. She was getting over-stocked, and so decided to buy a little pig and fatten him. She had a small hut put up in the corner of the garden for the purpose.

When the pig was about twelve or thirteen stone, she decided it should be killed. There was always a crowd of lads in at night, and she asked them if they would kill the pig. They agreed, and the day was fixed. Biddy had the pig fasting to be ready for the kill the next day. So the lads got a bright idea, they decided to steal the pig for themselves. Of course nobody had any meat at the time; they might have a bit on Christmas Day or some other special occasion. Generally pigs were sold to 'the big houses' and the money given back to them by way of rent.

In the dead of night, a few of the lads took the catch off the door and drove off the pig down the little lane and over the road. They killed it, cut up the meat and salted it and all that night.

The following morning when some of the lads called into Biddy, she was in a terrible state. 'The pig is gone,' says she. Of course they played the part, went out with her for a look, saying, 'He just got out. Ah, he'll be back.' But she, showing them the catch on the outside, explaining that he couldn't have got out of his own accord, sent them off in search of the pig, after she had given them each a drink.

Off they went, over the road, and came back again some time later. Couldn't find the pig! They had another drink, and off they went again. Weren't they hard men, knowing her reputation, and she supposed to be a witch?

The strange thing about this incident is that she went to her grave without ever knowing what happened that pig. Her insight and power was such that though she was able to help others, she was unable to use this gift in matters which concerned herself. It was one of the men who took part in the incident told me the story and he said he continued to go to her house each night with the rest of the lads, the same as if nothing had happened.[81]

She was a very sensitive person and never liked to be ridiculed. Giving her name to horses in the hope of acquiring luck was a regular occurrence, but this was not usually a good idea.

There was a man out the Tulla road near Ennis who used to keep a Flapper (race horse) and anxious that he would win in the races he called him 'Biddy Early'. She didn't like this, and her husband brought her in a horse and cart to the man's house.

'You have a race horse,' she said to him, 'and you call him Biddy Early. I don't like it. I am Biddy Early, and I want you to change the name.' But he only laughed and said he wouldn't. So she went away. At the next race meeting, the horse fell and broke his leg and was rendered useless.[82]

A man near O'Callaghan's Mills used to keep race-horses and didn't he call one o' the race-horses 'Biddy Early'. Biddy Early got to hear of it. 'Well,' says Biddy, 'that horse will never win a race.'

'Twas true for her. The horse was no use to him. She never won a race.[83]

There were times when she helped people even though she knew of their destiny in the years ahead, but she often warned those concerned of certain consquences.

A couple whose only son got very sick had tried

many doctors in an effort to obtain a cure. Someone suggested Biddy Early. 'If the doctors can't cure him, how can she?' he said. In any case he finally agreed. When he went to her she knew exactly what was the matter, and how the doctors had failed.

'He's the only child we have and would be a great loss to us,' said the man.

'If he lives now,' Biddy said, 'he will die when he'll be a greater loss.'

However, the distraught man wished that the boy should live. He did and grew to manhood. He got married and had a large family. And when all the children were quite young, he died, and was a great loss to his dependants.[84]

Throughout the years, she had brought business to her local village, Feakle, and to the surroundings, because many a long-distance caller had to remain overnight.

As the years wore on, long lines of carts, horse and carriages, continued to wait patiently along the rough road beside the 'humpy bridge.'

CHAPTER SIXTEEN

Though now over seventy years of age, she looked only about fifty or even less.[85]

One day, a young man just over thirty years of
age came into the yard, he was bent over with pain,
and had come to her for a cure. Biddy in her liber-
ated fashion said, 'I'll cure you if you'll marry me.'

He promised he would, and she cured him.

A report in *The Limerick Chronicle*, Thursday
Evening, 29 July 1869, states:

> We understand that a marriage of an extraordin-
> ary kind was celebrated this week in Limerick by
> one of the parish priests, that of an old woman
> known as 'Biddy Early' who resides near Tulla,
> and who, among the peasantry, has the reputa-
> tion of a witch or sorceress, who could cure all
> kinds of diseases, and such was her fascinating
> power over a fine young man. . . that she suc-
> ceeded in inducing him to become her fourth
> husband.[86]

The young man Biddy married was Thomas
Meaney. The pair were married in St Mary's Church,
Limerick, on 27 July, by Richard Scott, P.P., in
the presence of Cornelius McNamara and Susana
McNamara. And the certificate states that they
were married 'according to the Rites and Ceremon-
ies of the Roman Catholic Church'. Biddy's name
is given as 'Bridget Conners nee Flannery'. His age

is given as '40' and her's as being 'full'.[87]

Biddy continued her work for mankind, curing and helping those who sought her aid.

She herself was known to affirm that it was by the aid of divine power she effected her cures, but the clergy believed that it was through the agency of the devil they were accomplished. All agree in saying that she invoked the name of the Blessed Trinity in her cures.[88]

She never performed any cure, only in the name of the Holy Trinity.[89]

My mother was a next door neighbour of Biddy's. I always heard her say that she was a very good living woman in her private life and that she used to have her Rosary beads in her hands whenever she looked into the bottle.[90]

Like her first three husbands, Thomas enjoyed the company of the lads who came on *cuaird* and indulged himself in the spirits which were brought to the house. Just two months after their marriage, he again got sick. During the weeks which followed he had 'good' days and 'bad' ones. In spite of this he continued to drink.

After eight months' illness, he died at home in the cabin on 30 April 1870. Pat Meaney was again present at this death and according to the certificate, the death was 'uncertified'.[91]

At the age of seventy-two Biddy was a widow for the fourth time. And during the years which followed, she was often seen sitting by the fireside at the close of the evening 'telling her beads'.[92]

During these last years of her life her faculties and senses were slowly deteriorating. Tricks were being played on her, and children joked about her 'talking to her friends, the fairies', although any adult who tried to fool her still did not easily succeed. Then one day in the spring of 1874, she got very sick and was confined to bed. Her illness lasted a few weeks and during this time neighbours and well-wishers called to her bedside, and many continued to flock to her for 'a cure'.

A neighbour and life-long friend, Pat Loughnane, was a regular caller to her bedside. Anxious to bring about reconciliation between Biddy and the Church, he asked her if he would go for Fr Connellan, the parish priest in Feakle. Realising that her last moments were at hand, she consented.

The priest, being aware of the extraordinary power which this woman had had during her life, 'shook with fear' as he ascended the boreen.

A little table beside her bed had been covered with a white linen cloth on which rested two lighted candles and a little bowl of water. Biddy had the dark bottle in the bed beside her, wrapped in its red cloth.

The priest heard her confession, anointed her and reconciled her to the Catholic Church. He then called in those who remained in the other room, and some hours later, she breathed her last, in the afternoon of 22 April 1874. According to the death certificate, she had received no medical attention — the cause of death is listed as 'Debility', and Thomas Noonan is stated as having been 'present at death'.[93]

Fr Andrew Connellan[94] left the house and taking with him the famous bottle, he made his way across the short distance of a field, and hurled the bottle into nearby Kilbarron lake as Pat Loughnane and

Tom Minogue watched from the hillock outside the cottage. On returning he mounted his horse and rode away. Nobody ever heard whether Biddy told him to do this or whether he indicated to her that this would be his procedure.

The body of this controversial woman was laid out on the bed in which she died. A rosary bead found around her neck was left there -- 'in death as in life'.[95]

'Twenty-seven priests attended her funeral.'[96]

Nobody ever erected a headstone over her grave and, in fact, today the exact location is unknown.

In the aftermath of her death many priests, including Fr Dore (who had spent some time as parish priest of Feakle) and Fr Connellan, asked the people to pray for the repose of her soul.

The following Sunday, the parish priest spoke of her to his congregation. He said: 'We thought we had a demon amongst us in poor Biddy Early, but we had a saint, and we did not know it. She gave us information that will save both ourselves and our people to the end of time. She often got herself into trouble to save men of my own tribe.'

It was the general belief at the time she died that it was on her information the prayers after Mass were started.[97]

Linked with fact, mystery and legend, the story of Biddy Early's life will go on forever.

Before she died at Kilbarron side
She warned the neighbours firmly
That they must throw in the lough below
The Bottle o' Biddy Early.

Michael Hogan (1832-1899), the famous Bard of Thomond, wrote a poem entitled *The Fairy Hurling Match*. As a footnote to the poem, he has written,

The last of those fairy sybils who pretended acquaintance with the mystical lore of the spirit world, was the far-famed Biddy Early. . . The people held an emphatic belief in her powers and numberless are the stories told about the wonderful cures she performed. She was not a mercenary imposter for she'd take nothing, neither money nor value from any person whom she could not serve, and if the required service could be rendered she'd accept nothing but the meerest trifle, never surpassing a shilling. For patients came to her, even from the remotest parts of the country, and none never regretted a visit paid to 'poor honest Biddy' as she was affectionately termed by all who knew her. I once had an accidental opportunity of an interview with her. She predicted events in the far and near future of which I made private and special note. I was entirely sceptical in all she said, yet in course of time, I was astonished to experience the complete truth of her prophetic revelations.[98]

Twenty years after Biddy Early's death, Lady Gregory went to her cabin and was told by the woman who lived there then that years after her death people had continued to come looking for cures. The locals, from whom Lady Gregory collected stories about Biddy, termed her a great loss. When Lady Gregory returned home, her neighbours asked if Biddy was really dead!

Some years later the cottage fell into ruin, but in spite of this the fame of Biddy Early had continued to spread. People came not alone from other parts of Ireland, but also from other countries, especially America. So a local man, Dr Bill Loughnane, grandson of Pat Loughnane who had brought the priest to Biddy before she died, decided to rebuild the cottage exactly as it had been during her lifetime.

The doorway is the actual doorway from Biddy's house, and the fireplace and surround is the same [said Dr Loughnane]. A strange story relates to the dresser which is also Biddy's. When she died, a lady from Ayle, a great friend of Biddy's took the dresser to her own house. Perhaps Biddy had asked her to do this. In any case, many years later I attended this woman's son, who was then rather old, and one day I asked him if it was true that the dresser once belonged to Biddy Early. 'That is Biddy's dresser,' he told me, 'and do you see the drawer in the middle with the key hole, it's in that drawer Biddy kept her famous bottle.' My mother often told me about it.

Some years later this man was in hospital and the house was locked up, and it remained locked for years. Eventually when I was restoring the cottage, I thought it would be nice to have the exact dresser which once stood in Biddy's home, so I set about trying to get it.

Some time later we got the key, and a few friends of mine went one day with a tractor. The place was completely overgrown with briars and they had to cut their way in. The dresser was there, but the middle drawer where Biddy used to keep the bottle was missing. There was no sign of a break-in, no evidence that it had been taken by anybody from outside.

In any case, we brought the dresser to Biddy's cottage and nailed a board in front and painted it. So today Biddy's dresser stands in the cottage, minus the important drawer. We made several enquiries about the drawer, but nowhere could it be found. Who or what took that drawer still remains a mystery!'

Martin Ryan was working on a weekly radio programme for R.T.E. entitled *Munster Journal*. For one episode involving superstition and pishogery, he had done an interview with Dr Bill Loughnane on Biddy Early. He tells what happened.

Sunday morning I sent the tape to the studio to be transmitted on the following Friday night. Friday night came, and the programme opened — then the announcement came: 'We are unable to bring you *Munster Journal* just yet, we are sorry, but there will be a short delay.' Music played; again a while later, 'We are sorry, we are trying to make contact. . . ' and so on. In any case the programme did not come over the air that night.

I record over three hundred tapes a year, and this was the first time, and only time, that this happened to me. And seemingly there was no explanation why the programme could not and did not go on air that night.

Many people have tried to recover the bottle, including a man who came from England one time and claimed he had found it; apparently the evidence was against him.

Eamon O'Connor, who made a short television documentary and record of Biddy Early, had members of the Neptune Sub-Aqua Club attempt to recover her bottle from the lake on the centenary of her death, and he describes what happened.

The divers soon discovered that visibility was nil, and they could only feel their way through the dark bog-soft bottom. One of the divers came up with a dark bottle, and there was general excitment. This was the first time that a serious search of the lake had been made. The search recovered one small frying pan with two holes in it and no less than fifteen bottles. Sadly it is unlikely that Biddy's bottle is amongst the collection.[99]

On the night this documentary was to be transmitted on R.T.E. Television, there was a 'lightning strike' at the station, which occurred rather suddenly. Blame of the 'black out' was placed on the fact that a film on Biddy Early was to be shown.

W. B. Yeats often spoke of Biddy Early, according to Dermot MacManus (author of *The Middle Kingdom*), and comtemplated writing a book about her at one time. He called her 'the wisest of wise women'. Briefly he mentions her in a poem, where he speaks of Inchy Wood: 'Wise Biddy Early called the wicked wood. . .'

Finally, mention of an eye infection called blepharitis does not appear in any of the earlier writings (but has been spoken of in recent years) and for this reason, it has not been referred to, throughout this book.

Mr Fahy, whom Lady Gregory interviewed, said, 'She had no red eyes, but was a fresh clean-looking woman; sure any one might have red eyes when they'd got a cold.'[100]

Travelling on the train from Liverpool to London on an April afternoon in the mid-1880s, a young boy sat reading a book on palmistry when a distinguished looking man opposite him half humorously suggested he would like his palm read.

Great qualities of leadership were indicated by the well-marked line of Destiny in the man's hand. 'But why does it fade out so suddenly?' he asked the youth.

The lad pointed out where the line of Heart broke the line of Destiny before it faded out, indicating that it would be a woman. The man laughed, and said that was hardly likely. On parting he handed the young boy a card which read: 'Charles Stewart Parnell'.

Some years later the Irish leader fell in love with Kitty O'Shea and was cited in her divorce case which was the cause of his downfall.

The young man was William Warner of Bray, Co. Wicklow, who later became known as 'Cheiro', and was recognised as one of the greatest readers of his time of 'Your Line of Fate', predicting many events and disasters. (He died in 1936.)

Uri Geller, in view of many onlookers, vanished in Manhattan and seconds later reappeared in Ossining, New York. Nothing seems impossible as far as he is concerned, even bending metal at a distance with only the power of the mind.

Mathew Manning has shown that he can influence electrical or magnetic currents, start and stop machinery, and cause the appearance and disappearance of objects. He has in certain cases caused producers' tapes to be wiped clean, and even to disappear altogether.

In an experiment in Sweden, he 'blessed' one seed bed, 'cursed' another, and left a third alone. The beds were coded and not interferred with by anybody. One set came up lush, one hardly came up at all, and the third came up normally.

He admits that telepathy and clairvoyance come naturally to him.

Jeane Dixon has predicted such deaths as President John F. Kennedy's, Dag Hammarskjold's, and Marilyn Munroe's suicide. A devout Catholic, Jeane Dixon, through her psychic ability which she believes is a God-given talent to be used to help and benefit mankind, does not take any money for her predictions, only for her writings, broadcastings and other work.

Harry Edwards, assisted by Olive and George Burton, is probably the most successful spirit-healer in Britain today. He claims 40 per cent total cures and has healed many people given up as hopeless by doctors.

Lourival de Freitas performs 'psychic surgery' using knives and razor blades to operate, even beneath the eyelids, often removing a horney substance, yet no scarring takes place and the patient feels no pain. Cures by this 'healer' have been recorded.

Irene F. Hughes, who possesses psychic abilities, predicted the deaths of both President J. F. Kennedy and Robert Kennedy and Ted Kennedy's accident, among other predictions. When she was four years old she talked to what appeared to be a fairy, and which she now regards as a spirit. This spirit was to appear to her again in later years to tell her of her gift and has been her helping force in psychic predictions.

*   *   *

I cite the above events to illustrate that in today's more enlightened world, what was hitherto regarded as medieval superstition may now be regarded as a faculty which some individuals of the human race possess.

*   *   *

Biddy, of course, was a woman of her own time and, like the people of the superstitious age in which she lived, believed wholeheartedly in the fairies. The stories about her tell of her saying, 'Be careful of the fairy fort'; 'You crossed a fairy path'; or 'You went out on May Eve'.

There were various stories of the origin of the fairies. Some thought them to be the descendants of the Tuatha de Danaan, those powerful pre-Celtic magicians. Others considered them to be non-aligned angels during Lucifer's revolt against God: not good enough for heaven nor bad enough for hell, they were allowed to reside on earth. Some floated around in the air, others fell into the sea, but most remained invisible, often, it is said, whispering with wind-like voices. They added to their numbers by taking human beings. According to

Carolyn White, 'Although unseen, fairies still exist and are considered more numerous than the human race; more fairies are added to their number each year and few are ever taken away from them.'[101]

It was believed that Biddy talked with them all her life and did not contradict this impression; she is reputed to have said: 'This place between Finevara and Aughanish is the most haunted place in all Ireland'.[102]

Biddy Early lived in an age when learning was primitive, when interference by outside forces (like today's radio, television and constant rush) was slight. Telepathy — the transference of ideas, sensations and images — could be easily communicated because of the receptive mood or circumstances of the recipient.

Having studied some of the great mediums, psychics, clairvoyant people and witches in the world, I notice that they all speak of a power beyond themselves, of a Supreme Being: God. Most refer to a 'spirit' or 'control' which has helped and guided them and could be used for 'good' or evil purposes.

Psychic Douglas Johnson says he believes that all people have somebody from the other world who tries to help them along the path of life.

Perhaps 'The Good People', 'The Fairies' whom Biddy Early continually mentioned during her life were also spirits, which people with a 'super-normal power' speak of today.

Most of us have some grain of superstition. For instance, we will or will not do certain things because of a commonly held belief, and we would still fear spirits or any supernatural being.

Biddy Early, like most people, was aware of the good and evil force within her and knew, perhaps, from intuitive psychic vision that she could use her power for good, thereby being of tremendous help in her surrounding, deprived society.

Stories of her deeds would fill volumes, so it was not possible to use all, but by examining the stories a certain pattern emerges.

When a patient was sick at home, Biddy gave a bottle to the caller for him. If it broke the patient would die, and if it didn't he would be cured. I believe Biddy had psychic healing power. She knew whether or not it was destined for that patient to live or die, so when she handed the little bottle to the caller there was a living 'electric' transference, whereby she could either cause the bottle to be broken or to help cure the patient.

In the case of the priest (there are other similar cases), she asked for 'three thraneens' — a means of touch from her to the horse. Animals are more sensitive than human beings to the transference of thoughts. (A dog or horse will sense if you are afraid, sad, happy.) Through the priest, Biddy was able to immobilise the horse just as the Druids in early pagan Ireland used telepathic hypnosis with animals. The 'undoing' required a 'touch'. Here her power is comparable to a type of shaman or magician, where the essence requires a certain amount of concentration found only in a 'super-human' mind.

Telepathy and clairvoyance are closely linked. Biddy had this type of 'second-sight' whereby she knew the caller, and what the trouble was, and also she was aware of the outcome. In difficult cases she knew she would have to touch the patient in person, and did so on occasions to effect a cure.

Because neither Biddy nor the people around her understood the forces of the spirits, they accepted these phenomena as a manifestation of a Divinity greater than themselves. They celebrated His participation with rituals, like May Eve, November Night, and April Fool's Day.

What of the evil spells which were so rampant in nineteenth century Ireland? This requires an assessment of the forces of good and evil. The peasant folk were receptive to all types of spirits, and because of the great force of evil, very often it required a greater power to undo 'the spell' — a power like Biddy.

Dr Nancy Schmitz is a lecturer in folklore at Laval University in Quebec, and having spent many months in Ireland studying Biddy Early, she describes her as a *bean feasa*, 'wise woman' or 'woman of knowledge'. She places her as a mediator.

> The *bean feasa* was a type of go-between of the supernatural, the fairy world on the one hand and the ecclesiastical world on the other, establishing a sort of spiritual equilibrium in the community.
>
> The proper sphere of the *bean feasa*, however, was to counteract the results of spells cast by evil-wishers, and of fairy mischief.[103]

A supernatural cause was blamed for an undiagnosed ailment which would not respond to ordinary treatment. Dr Nancy Schmitz says,

> The belief in the power of the evil eye, or 'overlooking' by certain persons was strong. Biddy's extra-sensory powers were much in demand to

know the name of the one who had 'overlooked' the sick person.[104]

Biddy's powers are compatible with powers attributed to persons in societies having a strong relationship with nature, which was characteristic of Indo-European societies in Iron Age times, as it is in tribal societies of today.[105]

The misunderstanding of a power such as Biddy possessed was not confined to the uneducated peasant, but was worthy of respect by them. The clergy, on the other hand, sought a meaning for her actions in an unhallowed sense.

Dr Nancy Schmitz says:

She only respected the priests as long as they showed themselves deserving of respect. . . This casual attitude towards the ecclesiastical powers was occasioned by Biddy's knowledge that their condemnation of her was based on a mistaken assessment of her powers. Where the priests saw superstition and the presence of diabolical intervention, there was only psychic power, and no compact with any source of evil power. It must be stressed that the positive nature of Biddy's intervention is due to the character of the *bean feasa* which is not, in the proper sense of the term, a witch.[106]

Her bottle was merely an aid to concentration, a type of crystal ball, used to stimulate the subconscious for a difficult case. It made her more approachable, as the impression was given that the power was contained in the bottle rather than within her person.

Many things related to the supernatural world will possibly be never understood; being paranormal they cannot be tested by scientific means. All we can do is hope that an enlightened approach will make 'an unusual power' or 'a supernormal gift' more acceptable.

To sum up: I believe Biddy Early had 'a special gift' from a Supreme Power. She may have been visited by a supernatural spirits or spirits. She was 'a medium' between the ordinary peasants and their God.

The title that Biddy Early should be given rests in the hands of the individual reader.

NOTES

1. Listed in Griffith's Valuation of Tenements under Townland — Fahy.
2. M.B.C. Original document.
3. *The Midnight Court*, translated by Patrick C. Power, Mercier Press, Cork, 1971.
4. Dolly Steward, *Limerick Chronicle*, 17 October 1953 — *Limerick Leader* files.
5. *Our Boys*, November 1932; also T. Daly.
6. M.B.C.: Original document.
7. Mrs Leamey.
8. Literal translation: 'Without a drop of sense.'
9. M.P.B. & M.J.W.: Original manuscript.
10. Cathaireen was the old manuscript spelling given which created confusion—sorted with the help of P. Joyce and S. Murchuda.
11. Dolly Steward: Original manuscript.
12. Dolly Steward: Original manuscript.
13. A little field called Early's Haggard, also ruins of house is still to be seen in Carheen (property of Patrick Joyce).
14. James Hanrahan, Personal interview.
15. Behind where the County Clinic in Ennis stands today.
16. Report from Commissioners on Municipal Corporations in Ireland, p. 312. Also Report on Dept. of Local Gov. & Public Health — Act 11th and 12th George, cap. 30 (1771-2).
17. M.B.C.: Original manuscript (Thesis).
18. M.B.C.: Original manuscript (Thesis).
19. *Poitín* (Irish spelling).
20. In original documents, spelling Gurteenree for Gurteenreagh created confusion. Listed Griffith's Valuation: Townland — Gurteenreagh.

21. Dolly Steward: Original manuscript.
22. Dolly Steward: Original manuscript. Also M.P.B. & M.J.W.: Original manuscript.
23. Mrs Leamey.
24. S. 50, 1.a. 174. Folklore Dept. U.C.D.
25. M.P.B. & M.J.W.: Original manuscripts.
26. Dolly Steward: Original manuscript.
27. S. 36, 1.a.251-2: Folklore Dept. U.C.D.
28. Iml. 433, 11, 59: Folklore Dept. U.C.D.
29. S. 501, 1.a. 308: Folklore Dept. U.C.D.
30. S. 501, 1.a. 289: Folklore Dept. U.C.D.
31. Dolly Steward, *Limerick Chronicle* 17 October 1953 — *Limerick Leader* files.
32. The lake was, and is, more of a bog-hole.
33. The well can still be seen on the roadside below the cottage.
34. Correctly her home was in the townland of Dromore, but it is bordering on Kilbarron, which is the title of the habitation given to Biddy in the stories which refer to her; for this reason Kilbarron is used throughout the book.
35. Sean Browne (Shannonside).
36. M.P.W. & M.J.W.: Original manuscript.
37. *Travel Express (C.I.E.)*, August 1973.
38. Dolly Steward, *Limerick Chronicle*, 17 October 1953 — *Limerick Leader* files.
39. *Seaghan no Scuab*, a Gaelic play: *Our Boys*, November 1932.
40. Dolly Steward, Personal documents.
41. Iml. 382, LL 392. Folklore Dept. U.C.D.
42. Iml. 1011, LL 462-3. Folklore Dept. U.C.D.
43. Margaret Murphy, Personal Interview.
44. Though dead over 100 years, there are those who would not like to 'upset' Biddy, or draw her anger on them.
45. Iml. 615, 1.a. 305. Folklore Dept. U.C.D.
46. Iml. 707, 1.a. 164-7. Folklore Dept. U.C.D.

47. S. 510, 1.a. 111. Folklore Dept. U.C.D.
48. Lady Gregory, *Visions & Beliefs in the West of Ireland*, Colin Smythe Ltd, Bucks., Eng. 1970.
49. Ibid.
50. Dermot MacManus, *The Middle Kingdom*, Colin Smythe Ltd, Bucks, England, 1973.
51. Iml. 1013. LL 106. Folklore Dept. U.C.D.
52. Recording: Donncha Ó Dulaing, R.T.E. Sound Archives R.T.E., Eamon O'Connor; Film Documentary.
53. Iml. 1380, 1.a. 30. Folklore Dept. U.C.D.
54. J. Fitzgerald, Personal interview; also local tradition.
55. Nancy Schmitz, *Journal of the Folklore Institute*, Canada, Vol. XV, No. 3, 1977. From Ms 354, p. 348.
56. This was a different type of building from the House of Industry 1776. This Relief Workhouse stood where St Joseph's Hospital stands today.
57. S. 599, 1.a. 179. Folklore Dept. U.C.D.
58. Jim Fitzgerald, Personal interview.
59. S. 58, 1.a. 42. Folklore Dept. U.C.D.
60. Patrick Dollard, *Adventures of a Clare Moonlighter*. Patrick Dollard, 1965.
61. Ibid. Also accounts in Folklore Dept. U.C.D.
62. *Limerick Reporter & Tipperary Vindicator*, British Library Board, The British Library.
63. Ibid.
64. Ibid. Also other Clare, Limerick and Tipperary newspapers.
65. *Munster News,* British Library Board. The British Library.
66. Patrick Dollard, *Magic and Murder*. Patrick Dollard.
67. Iml 1013, 1.a. 111. Folklore Dept. U.C.D.
68. Margaret Murphy, Personal interview.
69. Margaret Murphy, Personal interview.
70. S. 604, 1.a. 29. Folklore Dept. U.C.D.
71. Jim Fitzgerald, Personal interview.
72. Dolly Steward, Personal documents.

73. Meda Ryan, Interview with Jim Fitzgerald. *Travel Express*, 1973. *Cork Holly Bough*, 1976.

74. Iml. 1380, 1.a. 30. Folklore Dept. U.C.D.

75. Sonny Walsh, Personal interview.

76. Ibid.

77. Donncha Ó Dulaing, R.T.E. Recording. *Sound Archives*, *R.T.E.*

78. Registered Death Certificate. Book No. 1 No. 202. Ennis Courthouse.

79. Patrick Dollard, *Magic & Murder*, Patrick Dollard.

80. Ibid.

81. Rev. P. Loughnane, P.P., Personal interview.

82. Ibid.

83. Iml. 433, LL 57-58. Folklore Dept. U.C.D.

84. Tommy Cassidy & Mary Ellen Cassidy, Personal Interview.

85. Mrs O'Brien.

86. *Limerick Chronicle. Limerick Leader* files. Newspaper report gives the name of Pat O'Brien from Glonagruss as the groom. Such a man did exist according to Griffith's Valuation. But according to the marriage records, the man she married was Thomas Meaney; no link with a Pat O'Brien could be found.

87. No. 461, St Mary's Church, Parish Records; Book No. 3, Entry No. 76, in No. 2 District County of City of Limerick. It reads Bridget Conners 'nee Flannery, rather than Bridge Flannery 'nee Conners. Spelling Conners rather than Connors.

88. S. 592, 1.a. 4. Folklore Dept. U.C.D.

89. Margaret Murphy, Personal interview.

90. Iml. 707, 1.a. 164. Folklore Dept. U.C.D.

91. Certificate, Book No. 1. Entry No. 317. Ennis Courthouse.

92. Saying the Rosary — local tradition.

93. Certificate No. 19. Book 2 Ennis Courthouse. The place of death is stated as Slievenore. But according to Griffith's Valuation, there were no Connors in Slievenore. Biddy had a relative in Slievenore. Possibly childhood associ-

ation (see Chapter Three) which may have been cause of incorrect entry. (Entry recorded by relative for cert.)

94. Fr Andrew Connellan, P.P. Feakle, died early Sept. 1874. (Five months after Biddy's death.)

95. Peggy Cox, Personal interview.

96. S. 510, 1.a. 111. Folklore Dept. U.C.D.

97. Ibid.

98. Michael Hogan, *The Lays and Legends of Thomond.* Michael Hogan.

99. *Film Documentary on Biddy Early.* Director, Eamon O'Connor.

100. Lady Gregory, *Visions & Beliefs in the West of Ireland*, Colin Smythe Ltd, Bucks., England, 1970.

101. Carolyn White, *History of the Fairies*, Mercier Press, Cork, 1976.

102. Dolly Steward, *Limerick Chronicle*, 17 October 1953 — *Limerick Leader* files.

103. Dr Nancy Schmitz, 'An Irish Wise Woman' in *Journal of the Folklore Institute*, Canada, Vol. XIV, No. 3, 1977.

104. Ibid.

105. Dr Nancy Schmitz, Personal letter.

106. Dr Nancy Schmitz, 'An Irish Wise Woman' in *Journal of the Folklore Institute*, Canada. Vol. XIV, No. 3, 1977.

BIBLIOGRAPHY

Alder, Marta, *My Life with the Gypsies*, Souvenir Press Ltd, London. 1960.

Danaher, Kevin, *Folktales of the Irish Countryside*, The Mercier Press, Cork. 1967.

——, *In Ireland Long Ago*, The Mercier Press, Cork. 1962.

——, *Irish Customs and Beliefs*, The Mercier Press Cork. 1964.

——, *Irish Country People*, The Mercier Press, Cork. 1976.

——, *The Year in Ireland*, The Mercier Press, Cork. 1972.

Dollard, Patrick, *Magic and Murder*, Patk. Dollard, Limerick.

Gregory, Lady, *Visions & Beliefs in the West of Ireland*, Colin Smythe Ltd, England. 1970.

Kennedy, Patrick, *Irish Fireside Folktales*, The Mercier Press, Cork. 1969.

——, *Legends of Irish Witches and Fairies*, The Mercier Press, Cork. 1976.

MacManus, Dermot, *The Middle Kingdom*, Colin Smythe Ltd, England. 1973.

Power, Patrick C., *The Midnight Court*, Translation (dual-language), The Mercier Press, Cork. 1971.

Psychic Magazine, Editors, *Psychics*, Turnstone Books. London.

St Clair, Sheila, *Psychic Phenomena in Ireland*, The Mercier Press, Cork. 1972.

Seymour, St John D., *Irish Witchcraft and Demonology*, E.P. Publishing Ltd, Yorkshire.

Underwood, Peter, *Into the Occult*, George H. Harrap & Co., London. 1972.

White, Carolyn, *A History of Irish Fairies*, The Mercier Press, Cork. 1976.

ACKNOWLEGEMENTS

While researching and writing this book, I received most generous help from many to whom I owe a debt of gratitude.

Seamus O Cathain and other staff members at the Folklore Department, University College Dublin; Noel Crowley, Clare County Librarian; Mary Moroney, Fionuala McNamara and Frances Hartley, Clare County Library Staff; Dolly Steward for personal help, encouragement and original documents; Don Kennedy and Peter Doyle, Sound Archives R.T.E.; Eamon O'Connor, Film Producer; Dr Nancy Schmitz, Laval University, Canada; Fr Ignasus Murphy; Sean O Murchadha; Gerry O'Connell; Fr P. Loughnane, P.P.; Mona Lysaght; Margaret Murphy; Noel Mulqueen; Patrick Joyce; Sonny Walsh; Jim Hanrahan; Dr Bill Loughnane, T.D.; Mary Pilkington; Mrs M. McManus; Martin Ryan, journalist; Mary M. Barry; Sean Browne, Shannonside Tourism; Mary Hynes; Peggy Cox; William O'Shaughnessy; Paddy Purcell; the proprietor of the *Clare Champion*, Flan Galvin (for use of files); Frank O'Dea, Editor *Clare Champion*, also staff members; Brendan Halligan, Editor *Limerick Leader*, and staff members; Gay Byrne and Research team, 'Gay Byrne Hour', R.T.E.; Walter McGrath, *Cork Holly Bough*; Tommy Cassidy, Mary Ellen Cassidy, and Peadar McNamara.

Grateful thanks is also due to the staffs at the Public Records Office, The British Library Board

Newspaper Library in London, The National Library and Trinity College Library in Dublin, Clare County Records Office, Limerick County Records Office, and the Keeper of Records at St Mary's Church Limerick.

A sincere word of thanks is due to the many who could not help directly, but took the trouble to write or telephone, explaining where information could be obtained.

NEWSPAPERS, PERIODICALS & RECORDINGS

The Clare Champion, The Clare Journal, The Limerick Leader, The Limerick Chronicle, The Munster News, The Limerick Reporter & Tipperary Vindicator, Original Manuscript from Dolly Steward, Our Boys, Ireland's Own, Cara — The Aer Lingus Magazine, Woman's Choice, The Cork Holly Bough, The Travel Express — C.I.E., The Journal of Irish Literature (Play on Biddy Early by Bryan Mc-Mahon), Journal of the Folklore Institute, Canada (Study by Dr Nancy Schmitz), Griffith's Valuation, List of Electors — Public Records, Register of Freeholders, Death Certificates, Marriage Certificates, Original Manuscript — M.P.B. & M.J.W. — Thesis, Government Report, Grand Jury Presentments, Manuscripts of Folklore Department, University College, Dublin, R.T.E. Recordings, Eamon O'Connor's recording & film documentary script, several hand-written and type-written accounts and letters, many personal interviews.

111

LEGENDS OF IRISH WITCHES AND FAIRIES
Patrick Kennedy

From Patrick Kennedy's early youth he felt a deep interest in stories and legends which were peculiar to Ireland. All our superstitions and a great part of our legendary lore, have been handed down to us from our ancestors and Kennedy's dearest wish was that their memory should not fade from the minds of the people. He recorded these fascinating tales of the occult as they were told to him by the people around the fireside.

FOLKTALES OF THE IRISH COUNTRYSIDE
Kevin Danaher

A delightful collection of stories of giants, of ghosts, of wondrous deeds, queer happenings, of fairies and the great kings of Ireland who had beautiful daughters and many problems.

GENTLE PLACES AND SIMPLE THINGS
Kevin Danaher

These essays are about the beliefs and traditions of tinkers and highwaymen, of crickets and witchcraft, of fairies and ghosts; they are all here, and many more, treated with understanding and respect, but never with condescension.

IRISH COUNTRY PEOPLE
Kevin Danaher

Irish Country People is simply one fascinating glorious feast of folklore and interesting sidelights of history recorded without a fraction of a false note or grain of sentimentality. The topics covered in the twenty essays range over a wide field of history, folklore, mythology and archaeology. There are discussions about cures, curses and charms; lords, labourers and wakes; names, games and ghosts; prayers and fairy tales.